A SHEARWATER BOOK

The Forgotten Founders

THE FORGOTTEN FOUNDERS

Rethinking the History of the Old West

Stewart L. Udall

Foreword by
David M. Emmons

Island Press / SHEARWATER BOOKS
Washington • Covelo • London

A Shearwater Book
Published by Island Press

Copyright © 2002 Island Press

All rights reserved under International and Pan-American Copyright
Conventions. No part of this book may be reproduced in any form or
by any means without permission in writing from the publisher: Island
Press, 1718 Connecticut Avenue, N.W., Suite 300, Washington, DC
20009.

Shearwater Books is a trademark of The Center for Resource Economics.

Library of Congress Cataloging-in-Publication Data
Udall, Stewart L.
  The forgotten founders : rethinking the history of the old West /
Stewart L. Udall.
      p.   cm.
Includes bibliographical references and index.
  ISBN 1-55963-894-x (pbk. : alk. paper)
  1. West (U.S.)—History. 2. West (U.S.)—Historiography. I. Title.
F591 .U45 2002
978—dc21   2002005951

British Cataloguing-in-Publication Data available

Book design by Brighid Willson

Printed on recycled, acid-free paper

Manufactured in the United States of America
09 08 07 06 05 04   8 7 6 5 4

FOR LEE
My companion and collaborator
of fifty-four years, whose judgments about people,
words, and human events were so fine.

Contents

PART III
Violence in the Old West:
Correcting the Record

Removing the Barnacles

DAVID M. EMMONS

It has been said that the past is a different country, that they do things differently there. From the perspective of the spring of 2002, and for reasons that do not require explanation, the past now seems not only different but otherworldly. And I refer not to the distant past, to the Age of Andrew Jackson, say, but to what is still called modern America, and to the Age of Presidents John F. Kennedy and Lyndon Johnson. To take one specific event, consider the presidential election of 1960. A case could be made that we were a simpler people then, and a bit simple-minded. Certainly both descriptions could have been applied to me. I had just turned twenty-one and was in my senior year at the University of Colorado. I remember the early season blizzard I drove through on my way from Boulder to Denver to cast my first ballot in a presidential race.

I voted for Kennedy. As a Catholic from a working-class family, this was almost a sacred calling. But there was also an important ideological, or at least psychological, component to my vote. Richard Nixon belonged to the Age of Dwight D. Eisenhower. We know now that Eisenhower's record on civil rights was both exemplary and courageous and that, of all the cold war presidents, he would be the least bellicose. But we didn't know that then. All I knew at the time was that Ike was outdated and that Nixon was his heir, different only in terms of chronological age. Kennedy was young, passionate, and brave and would be surrounded and counseled by others like himself.

There was even talk that Kennedy would appoint a westerner as secretary of the interior. That in itself was hardly newsworthy. Westerners were always being appointed secretary of the interior as a sop to the natural resource industries. But this time the talk was of a western *conservationist.* I thought I knew what conservationists were, and I liked them. As a western Catholic with a familial and reflexive attachment to the Democratic Party and a developing belief that something of the natural West should be saved, I would have driven through hell to vote for Kennedy.

Much has happened since then. The Kennedy promise was cut short and was quite likely unattainable anyway. But a part of it survived, even flourished. It flourishes still. The new president selected Stewart Udall of Arizona as his secretary of the interior. Udall was as young and passionate and courageous as the most idealistic of us could have wished for, and he gave Kennedy and later Johnson very wise counsel on the preservation and management of America's natural resources and treasures—counsel that, I would now argue, they too seldom heeded. It was Udall who coined the term "the myth of superabundance." It was a felicitous phrase, and he sold it to both Kennedy and Johnson and to most of the American people who were listening. But with the conspicuous and important exception of the Wilderness Act of 1964, the substance of what he was getting at has fared less well. To Udall as much as to any other of his generation goes the credit for the beginnings—faint, to be sure, but discernible—of a new environmental awareness and ethic. As remarkable, this new ethic came from a westerner and in the cadence and parlance of the West. More than forty years later, in this different country, Udall, much changed and young now only in spirit, is still passionate and brave and still providing us with wise counsel. He is for me the perfect and enduring legacy of the Kennedy promise.

The Forgotten Founders: Rethinking the History of the Old West is Stewart Udall's ninth book. I want to discuss it in the company of two of his others, *The Quiet Crisis,* a history of the conservation movement but also a love song to the West and its people, written in 1963, and *The Myths of August: A Personal Exploration of Our Tragic Cold War Affair with the Atom,* finished in 1994. Each of these two earlier books is intensely personal, and each reflects its author's deep commitments. They are, however, strikingly different in temper and essence. *The Quiet Crisis* is the work of a hopeful idealist; *The Myths of August* is darker, the work of someone disappointed at best, disillusioned at worst. Something happened to Udall—and the rest of us—between 1963 and 1994. My reference is not just to assassinations, futile wars, and frustrated dreams of racial peace. Udall experienced all of that more directly and personally than most, and the events of those years affected him deeply. But there was another experience that may have been even more determinative and was certainly more important in guiding him toward both *The Myths of August* and *The Forgotten Founders.*

In the 1970s, Udall began his decades-long legal representation of those he calls the "downwinders," Navajo Indians and others who were victims of the U.S. government's reckless testing of atomic weapons. To represent them well required that he learn more about the government's atomic affairs. Not to put too fine a point on it, he discovered that the government had lied and that many of those lies had been told by men for whom he'd had great respect and affection. Listen to what he had to say: "Almost against my will, I finally concluded that Roosevelt and Stimson, two of my political heroes, had covered up their participation in [the] decision" to use saturation bombing on Japanese civilians. As for Kennedy and Johnson, they were guilty of "political gamesmanship." Kennedy's inaugural, initially thought a call to sacrifice, was in fact a call to arms, an "overblown commitment," leading directly to the tragedy of the Vietnam War.

More generally, he grew convinced that government leaders had turned the post-Hiroshima "atomic age into the most mythologized . . . in American history, . . . filled with histrionic half-truths and fictions promulgated by . . . official spokesmen." And these were no minor deceptions. Udall was characteristically blunt: "During the sad history of the atomic age and the Cold War, our . . . leaders betrayed [our] institutions and thus the American people." Their lies were gross distortions—Big Lies, Udall called them, warning us that "once a Big Lie gains sway over a nation . . . it strangles creative dissent." He knew very well his own susceptibility. In *The Quiet Crisis*, he wrote of "the fashioning of an almost self-renewing source of energy by . . . physicists who uncovered the edge of an infinite dynamo . . . and allayed our fears of fuel shortage once and for all." His reference was to breeder reactors—magical (and, as it turned out, mythical) devices that not only would create atomic energy but also would simultaneously breed new sources of that energy. He may well have meant to describe himself in writing that "when a person's outlook has been shaped by illusions, disenchantment is a gradual process."

Gradual perhaps, but in his case, sure and decisive. In 1963 in *The Quiet Crisis*, Udall held up the federal government as central to developing a new national land ethic. He has not entirely abandoned that notion, but the faith he had in the government diminished as he watched the atomic establishment and its political and journalistic shills deceive and dissemble, whether promoting the concept of breeder reactors, combating the Soviet threat, or justifying the bombing of Hiroshima and Nagasaki. The easy confidence, which is to say the naïveté, of *The Quiet Crisis* would be replaced by a different, more suspicious, interpretative frame.

Udall's great strength, however, is that his disenchantment is only partial. There are always people of vision and honor—including the majority of settlers Udall discusses in *The Forgotten Founders*—and from them and from his own considerable resources he draws his apparently inexhaustible supply of hope. One from whom he took lessons in hope was Russian physicist and dissident Andrei Sakharov. Udall's comparison of Sakharov and the bumptious American physicist Edward Teller in *The Myths of August* is brilliant and chilling. But what struck me particularly was Udall's description of Sakharov's credo and how closely it resembled Udall's own. Sakharov believed that "the moral capital one acquired should be spent, not sequestered. . . . Each individual should seize any opportunity to sow seeds of change."

For Udall, what clearly needed changing were the myths of American history. His concern is not with the stories a community tells of itself. These help center a people and enable them to make sense of their lives. He reserves his hostility for purposeful and self-serving lies, whether about atomic power—the inventions of August designed to suit the atomic establishment—or, as in *The Forgotten Founders*, the overblown and ahistorical emphasis on a "Wild West" filled with unlikely, if not entirely imaginary, swashbucklers to suit an eastern (or Hollywood) establishment. These myths are not only purposeful distortions; they also have a remarkably long shelf life. I recall a conversation in which Udall likened them to barnacles on a ship, encrusted and securely fastened. He is determined to remove them. The myths of August provided an ideological justification for increasing budgets. Western myths, by emphasizing individualism (always, it seemed, of the rugged variety), provided eastern corporations with a uniquely American antidote to any form of collectivism. And note how similar the myths are and how frequently they share characters: John Wayne wore both a cowboy hat and a green beret; Ronald Reagan was both a western player and a cold warrior. And who could forget Slim Pickens in *Dr. Strangelove,* waving his Texas hat, whooping out his bronc-busting yells, and riding the Bomb to oblivion? The Wild West meets the nuclear winter.

Udall believes that too many of the stories that attend and define the "Wild West" are historical illusions created by frustrated dreamers and opportunistic dream makers. Bernard De Voto was the best example of the former, and Udall is unsparing in his criticism of him and his hopelessly romanticized and condescending attempts at history. In this, Udall belongs among the New West historians who have rescued an important field of historical inquiry from those who would render it irrelevant by rendering it false. He differs from some of those historians in his concern for process as well as place—for the constantly shifting frontier as well as the geographically fixed West—but even on this matter he certainly does not stand alone.

There is, in fact, on this point as on others, an important and shared belief that aligns Udall with the larger world of historical scholarship: the frontier, for Udall, as for the New West historians, is not a line of war. He uses the word "frontier," but not as Frederick Jackson Turner did, in a culturally loaded way. Indeed, I think one of the most important sections of *The Forgotten Founders* is that in which he insists that conflict with native peoples often resembled murderous assaults on civilians more than war, and that to refer to these conflicts as war allowed (and allows) Americans to escape moral responsibility for the actions taken in their name. The capture of Guadalcanal and the Battle of the Bulge took place during wars. The massacres at Wounded Knee and Sand Creek did not; they were acts of violence and terror. The New West historians, I believe, would agree with Udall on this point, just as they would agree with his insistence that, with the exception of violence against native peoples, the West was not the wild and rambunctious place the mythmakers would have us believe. This is a very subtle and important argument.

Udall substitutes for the mythical Wild West an Old West, the home place for those he calls the wagon families: men and women, rural and urban, in industrial and agricultural settings, who came, camped, settled, and stayed. But that means as well that his West was not a corporate colony or a government creation. It was not the satrapy of eastern capital, the ward of federal bureaucrats, or the endgame of some global system. Nor was it a Hollywood-style jousting ground for gold seekers and gunfighters. Udall's westerners would not have recognized these descriptions. The West, for them, was simply the place where they and their families were from, and from which they took their identity and their character.

His anger at those who deny this truth is genuine, partly because it arises out of his own affection for and familiarity with western places. He loves those places—the landscapes and the weather, the towns and the farms. But mostly he loves the people who *settled* them, from American Indians to Franciscan friars to Mormon pioneers. These people did not "win" the West or even subdue it. Their watchwords, and his, were "amity, not conquest; stability, not strife; conservation, not waste; restraint, not aggression." The people Udall knows and loves best embraced the West and fashioned their lives in accordance with its seasons, rhythms, and laws. As he puts it:

Seen whole, the West was not "conquered" by feats of marching armies. American hegemony was established on the ground, not by decisions of far-off political leaders. In large measure, the West's future was shaped by courageous men and women who made treks into wilderness and created communities in virgin valleys.

He knows of the high rate of population transiency in the West, knows that the persistence rates for western towns and villages were very low. But he wants to talk about those who stayed the course. The flurry of comings and goings they witnessed was like the wind and the coyotes—part of western life, but not its essence. History, he insists, is about continuity as well as change, stability as well as motion, gentleness as well as violence.

There's another barnacle he intends to remove. At a time when secularism has come to assume the dimensions and some of the forms of a religion, this barnacle has a particularly tight hold. Brigham Young, Archbishop John Baptist Lamy, Father Pierre-Jean De Smet, and their followers, Udall points out, were more important than any legion of romanticized mountain men, cavalry officers, or others of the manifestly destined. This is not an easy point to make, especially among those who assume that because religion is of no importance to them, it cannot have been of any importance to anyone. For these individuals—and there are many western historians among them—religion is reduced to a bizarre form of collective behavior that can be understood in a historical context only as it answered material needs. As an approach to the study of the past, this cannot capture the self-understanding of a people who believed in and lived a life beyond that in which the historians find and study them. The simple fact is that until rather recently and for the vast majority of the world's people, including those who settled the American West, religion was central to both their material and their spiritual lives.

It connected them—to one another and to the places where they lived. It defined who they were.

Udall was raised a Mormon. I don't know whether he is still a member of the Mormon Church; I never asked him. Member or not, believer or not, his respect for who the Mormons are and what they did is obvious on these pages. He refers to them often, but his attention is not unwarranted. They are iconic representations of the western settler—the forgotten pioneers. Udall likes the phrase that anthropologist Janet Finn uses to describe the women and men who lived and worked in mining towns: they "crafted the everyday." The Mormon settlers did that, too—and they were master craftsmen. They epitomized what in *The Myths of August* he calls the "most intrinsic values of all—sharing, caring, and cooperation."

As I read Udall's descriptions of the "ground-floor" Mormons, many of them members of his family, who landed in, and fixed themselves to, the canyon lands of Utah and Arizona, I was reminded of what always seemed to me an oddity of western history: western historians deal with the Mormons—they could hardly not—but they deal with them as set-asides, something vaguely alien and out of place. Mormon history is seen as both a category separate to itself and a part of American religious history, not a subcategory of western history. The reasons are obvious, and Udall suggests them throughout this book: the barnacled West was a place of wild and reckless individuals—mostly men—seekers after the main chance, explorers, exemplars of America's Manifest Destiny mythology. The Mormons don't fit neatly in this distorted historical taxonomy. Udall—as did Wallace Stegner—has a wider view. Stegner called Mormons "the most systematic, organized, disciplined and successful pioneers in our history." Udall agrees, hence their very substantial role in his history, which shows us the importance of another West.

They were successful pioneers because of their quite extraordinary sense of community. They counted on one another to give
meaning and substance to their lives. Udall and I have talked frequently of one of the more unlikely pairings in western history:
the Irish Catholics of industrial Butte, Montana, and the Mormon pioneers on the farms and ranches of Utah and Arizona.
Both groups demanded and demonstrated an almost tribal alle-
giance. They weren't just clannish; they stuck together with fero-
cious loyalty. To be sure, there were some unlovely aspects of
communities this tightly bound. They could be prickly and
defensive, almost to the level of collective paranoia. Remarkably
inclusive and embracing with "the elect," they were just as exclu-
sive and suspicious toward all others. They judged harshly—both
themselves and the "gentiles," however defined. One might wish
they had been more tolerant, but for all that, how remarkable was
their support for one another!

There is no doubt that Udall perceives himself as not just the
descendant of such as these but also a full participant in their
community. To put it somewhat differently, he knows that true
community has a temporal as well as a spatial component, that it
extends across generations as well as space. It is this understanding that propels him toward what I think is the most moving and
evocative part of the book, and one of the defining moments of a
life well and fully lived. Stewart Lee Udall is not just the descendant of Mormon pioneers. He is the great-grandson of John D.
Lee, the man held accountable for the Mountain Meadows massacre. Udall's account of John Lee and the massacre is searing,
unforgettable. But so was what Udall did in 1989 and 1990. He
helped to organize a meeting of Mormons and the families of
those Arkansans who had died at Mountain Meadows more than
130 years earlier.

The gathering took place just outside Cedar City, Utah, not

far from the Mountain Meadows. The president of the Mormon Church was there, as were other Mormon dignitaries. They were joined by the descendants of those who had died at the hands of a Mormon militia. There were speeches; a monument was unveiled. But what will endure for me was Udall's poem, which he recited to those gathered at the site. It was a plea for forgiveness, and the pain that attended its writing was palpable. How, he asks, does one "forgive unforgivable acts"? "I wept at the ceremony," he relates, "and I still weep every time I read the names" of those who died. This poem was far more than a literary exercise. It was an act of atonement for sins committed by his ancestors. And for me, nothing explains Stewart Udall as surely as this simple act of penance.

The Udall of 2002 is vastly different from the one of 1963. He has absorbed countless blows, and like all the brave and thoughtful men of his generation, he has been scarred by them. He didn't just mature between 1963 and 2002; he was battered and hardened. But he never succumbed to cynicism, and he never whined. Even his anger is marked by the same essential sweetness he showed in 1963. As he asked for forgiveness for Mountain Meadows, so has he forgiven. But he has not forgotten, and he wants mightily for Americans to realize that "we cannot understand our history unless we see it whole and tell it true."

The Forgotten Founders, in the final accounting, is about connectedness, about fixing and holding to both place and community. It is about steadfastness and tenacity, those elements of *settled* western society that have not changed. Those were the values that sparked and sustained *The Quiet Crisis* and the environmental movement it helped to inspire. Udall didn't put himself on that list of timeless and immutable western elements. But he is as essential, as elemental, in his westernness as too little rain, so I will add him now. What was once said about his great-grandfather David Udall could also be said of him: "He . . . lives in fearless simplicity. . . . He does not know the first element of scheming and he abhors debt. . . . No man could be more industrious, frugal, and honest." I can't speak to Udall's financial frugality and abhorrence of debt, but the rest of this tribute certainly applies. And let it be noted, as Sakharov did, that there is moral as well as financial capital and that debt and frugality can take forms other than those of the accountants. I return to Udall's act of atonement at the Mountain Meadows. He paid off a debt. As for frugality, he has demonstrated with his writings that we should not waste the truths history has given us but should continue to use and learn from them. His life, not just this book, is a reminder of that.

Preface

"So, out in our West, artists are trying to run their eyes clear of mythic and legendary cobwebs, and see . . . straight to the beating meaningful heart of things."

—William Kittredge

The course of history is elusive, and there are times when experience provides insights as important as those found in books. I had the good fortune to spend my formative years in a farm village on Arizona's Colorado Plateau, a village founded in the 1870s during the last phase of colonizing in the American West. In the 1920s, this was obviously no longer a frontier setting, but as a child growing up there I gleaned illuminating details of the past from old-timers, and the community itself was still redolent with remnants of frontier life.

Where frontiering is concerned, the journals and diaries of pioneer families—and the personal reminiscences of their children—are usually invaluable sources of information. I absorbed this truth when, as a young adult, I studied the stories of great-grandparents who had come to the West as settlers in the 1840s and 1850s. Knowledge I gained about their lives and the milieu in which they functioned enlarged my understanding of the fundamental forces that shaped the initial phase of western settlement.

When I started to write this book, I realized how experiences of my own youth threw light on the limitations nature and geography had imposed on the West's early settlers. The history and current circumstances of St. Johns, Arizona, the isolated village on the Little Colorado River where I grew up, helped me understand the motives, disciplines, and constraints that had influenced human behavior on the frontier.

Men and women of my generation who grew up on farms or ranches or in small towns where there was no electricity, and where horses and mules provided the energy needed to till fields, gather wood, and harvest crops, are familiar with conditions that dictated the daily lives of early settlers. We remember the outdoor chores the children had to perform to help provide the food and fuel each household needed, and we recall how important horses, milk cows, chickens, calves, and pigs were to the sustenance of our families.

Such memories also encompass participation in community activities such as cleaning canals and working alongside carpenters and masons who were building churches, schools, and public meeting places. Wallace Stegner underscored the essence of communal cooperation in the Old West when he observed, "The Mormons discovered what the cliff-dwellers had discovered centuries before, that the only way to be a farmer in the Great Basin and on the desert plateaus of the Colorado River watershed [where dams had to be built and miles of irrigation ditches had to be dug] was to be a *group farmer*."

Stegner's apt generalization described not just the Mormon experience but also the experience of native peoples and pioneer families in the semi-arid areas of the West stretching from the Southwest to Montana and eastern Washington. As my horizon widened, I developed a boundless admiration for the Protestants who trekked across half the continent to Oregon and for the

Spanish Catholics who established a pastoral colony in New Mexico in 1598, two decades before the Pilgrims came ashore in Massachusetts.

Individuals who grew up in small towns many decades ago also recall how face-to-face patterns of daily life tended to teach tolerance and soften human conflicts. Orderly behavior is enhanced when each individual knows everyone in the community and social and religious observances foster mutual respect. It is a social truism that citizens police themselves when their lives intermingle. In my town, for example, the beloved midwife (Charlotte Sherwood) and the high school music teacher long occupied a more vibrant place in our communal life than the sheriff—and codes of conduct inculcated by churches had a stronger influence on behavior than laws enacted by a distant legislature.

Later, first as a congressman and then as secretary of the U.S. Department of the Interior, I was given a spacious vantage point to learn more about the land and water policies that had governed the lives of western pioneers and their progeny. When President John F. Kennedy invited me to serve in his cabinet in 1961, I felt the need for counsel from individuals who had special insights concerning the country's resources and the story of its land use and people. To fill this gap, I invited writers I admired to come to Washington, D.C., and provide guidance for me and my associates. Two new friends who became inspiring tutors were Alvin Josephy Jr. and Wallace Stegner.

Stegner's basic convictions about western history were derived not from digging in archives but from the life he had lived in various western settings. To him, the frontier was not an abstract subject. As a youngster, he had participated in his family's struggle to subjugate raw land and help create a community in a hardscrabble area of Saskatchewan.

Stegner urged me to write a book about the land-and-people story of the United States, and the outline he left on my desk as he departed became the basis for *The Quiet Crisis,* which was published in 1963. The research animated by that project widened my understanding of the nation's history and illuminated its flawed record of resource management.

I learned from our conversations that Stegner had enormous respect for the competence and tenacity of the first-generation families who settled in the West. Above all, he admired the spirit of self-sacrifice and cooperation that enabled those pioneers to create lasting, cohesive communities in the Old West. These talks helped me begin to recognize that there were gross distortions blurring the vision of most Americans about the settlement of the Old West.

A critic of gold rushers, boomers, and other self-styled rugged individualists whose motives were materialistic, Stegner expressed contempt for the historical distortions generated by the legion of writers and filmmakers who had transformed the Old West into the Wild West. *The Gathering of Zion,* his book about the Mormon hegira, contained no references to guns or gunplay. "For a while," he once said, "the only kind of literature was Louis L'Amour. It was Colt revolver literature made up of interchangeable parts."

Alvin Josephy Jr. had already won distinction as a historian when he became my collaborator in 1963. An easterner who had a love affair with the West, Josephy had blown fresh air into a cliché-infested room of American history. *The American Heritage Book of Indians,* which he edited in 1961, and *The Patriot Chiefs,* published the same year, constituted a frontal attack on the stereotypes that had warped mainstream American thinking about native peoples and their cultures.

By presenting American history from an Indian point of view,

Josephy forced his readers to recognize the enriching contributions native peoples had made, and were making, to American
life. He had a passionate interest in the story of western settlement and an unerring eye for the hubris and betrayals that had
stripped Indians of their ancestral lands and undermined their
culture. Josephy was a cogent polemicist, and within a decade
many of his ideas would be embodied in new Indian policies.

My crash course of study at Interior quickened my interest in
the history of the American West and encouraged me to ponder
the patterns of its settlement and the turning points of my
region's history. A lifetime of observations has convinced me that
an effort must be made to clear the record and present a balanced
view of European settlement. My aim in writing this book was to
pay homage to the authentic heroes and heroines of the first
phase of western settlement and to rescue the primal story of
their achievements from the pallid margins of history where
twentieth-century entertainers and mythmakers have ignomin-
iously dumped them.

The Forgotten Founders

How the West's Settlers Were Ousted from Their Olympian Ledge

We all know the standard images—the six-gun-toting sheriff, the gunfight at the corral or watering hole, telegraph relays and passengers arriving in town after a long train or stagecoach ride, fisticuffs in the saloon, and gold seekers trying to get the jump on the claims of others. In this whirl, as we see it on film or read it in popular accounts of the West's history, remarkably little attention is given to the pioneering work of the early settlers, who did so much to establish permanent communities in a wild, inhospitable land. If the settlers appear at all, it is as extras for an attack on a wagon train snaking across the landscape or as the audience for a gunfight or a posse for a pursuit. Much of the confusion that has made it difficult to comprehend the achievements of the West's settlers would be dispelled if the history of that primal period were divided into two distinct epochs. The first would encompass the time through the founding of communities by wagon-train families. The second would begin when railroads brought elements of the industrial revolution into the West.

The European entrada commenced in 1598 when a Basque nobleman, Juan de Oñate, led more than 200 families northward

1,000 miles and established a Spanish agrarian settlement in a
beautiful valley in northern New Mexico. Carrying their posses-
sions in wooden-wheeled wagons and carts, this vanguard traveled into a remote heartland of what is now the United States of
America twenty-two years before the storied Pilgrims landed in
Massachusetts. Juan de Oñate's group was followed over the next
two centuries by other Spanish pioneers from the south who created additional settlements in the Southwest and in northern
California. Nearly 250 years would elapse before wagon parties
entering from the East would cross the Great Plains and begin to
populate other regions of the American West.

This saga of western settlement constitutes a remarkable
chapter in American history. Whether these pioneers were motivated by religious faith or by a desire to possess free land, their
ventures entailed uncommon courage, lasting month after
month, mile after mile. The shallow, hastily dug graves that lined
the wagon roads were signposts of that courage, and its fiber was
attested by the risky assumption that families who arrived in
midsummer could erect rude habitations and ward off hunger by
harvesting enough foodstuffs before the onset of winter. We
might call these Pilgrims Trekkers.

A second category of immigrants, many of them more recent
arrivals from northern Europe, also belong in the pantheon of
Old West pioneers. These were the families who struggled into
expanses of the Great Plains and established farms and communities on the prairies of the Middle Border before or soon after
the Civil War. These pioneers plowed treeless grasslands in
Kansas, Colorado, Nebraska, and the Dakotas, where erratic
weather often blighted crops and hopes.

Like their counterparts who traveled to the Far West, these
subsistence farmers brought all their belongings in wagons and
relied on their horses, cows, pigs, and chickens for sustenance.

Their day-to-day struggle on this demanding frontier is a story of adversities ranging from recurring droughts to occasional raids by natives who resisted incursions into their homelands. These pioneers might be called the Prairiebusters.

The world of these Spanish and Anglo-Saxon Trekkers and first-generation Prairiebusters was notably different from the West of a later time. After the Civil War, the region was changed profoundly when railroads brought in machines and products of the industrial age. The table on the following page summarizes the major technological, cultural, and economic differences that came to characterize the two eras.

In this book, I attempt to provide a perspective within which the achievements of the West's European founders can be seen, once again, as a distinctive, glorious episode of American history. I begin with the first settlers—the American Indians—to establish the larger context. I then turn to early settlement by peoples of European origin before taking on a range of areas in which the past of the early settlers has been distorted or obscured.

Indian Settlements

A study of American settlement must begin with the recognition that some native peoples developed impressive societies in various parts of the continent, the West included. Ignorance long enveloped this subject because the minds of most Americans were cluttered with stereotypes of warlike, primitive savages who hindered the civilizing work of those of European descent. In the 1960s, Alvin Josephy Jr. began writing and editing books that tell a different story. Josephy combed the archives for old documents, paintings, and photographs and produced texts that, by presenting history from an Indian point of view, revealed the lasting contributions natives had made to the nation's history.

The Old West	*The Post-Railroad West*

Living Conditions

• Agrarian character prevails; most settlers live in small villages in previously untrammeled environments.	• A cash economy develops as railways link communities to national markets.
• Urbanization is slow; the only nascent cities are Salt Lake City, Denver, Omaha, Portland, and a few others.	• Cities grow rapidly when railroads reach southern California and the Puget Sound.
• Families grow or hunt most of their own food; light is provided by candles and fireplaces.	• Railroads bring staple foods, household goods, cans of kerosene, and lamps.

Transportation and Commerce

• Animals provide energy to propel wagons, plows, and carriages.	• Big resource development begins as railroad spur lines to remote sites are built and the West begins supplying copper, lumber, and other resources to national markets.
• Heavy wagons pulled by draft animals import small grist mills and other rudimentary machines; stagecoaches and pony express riders offer mail service.	• By linking mainline communities to the outside world, railroads and the telegraph unify the nation.

Energy

• Draft animals do heavy farmwork and bring wood supplies to homes.	• Railroads expand energy use by importing coal, kerosene, and turbines to generate electric power.

Craftwork

• Artisans and blacksmiths make most of the settlers' furniture and tools by hand.	• Railroads bring in machines to manufacture furniture and tools.

Guns

• Settlers typically own only single-shot muzzle-loading rifles, which they use to harvest wild game.	• After the Civil War, six-gun pistols, shotguns, and modern quick-action rifles developed during the war become available.

Cowboys

• Cows and other animals are herded by family groups.	• With the advent of cattle cars that can transport range animals to eastern slaughterhouses, railroads make large-scale ranching highly profitable. Herders called cowboys come into existence when ranchers need full-time help to manage their cattle.

Josephy's work, stretching from his groundbreaking *The Patriot Chiefs: A Chronicle of American Indian Leadership* (1961) to his masterful, hemispheric *500 Nations: An Illustrated History of North American Indians* (1994), is so cogent that a latecomer can only compose something that buttresses Josephy's core contentions. In chapter 1 of this book, to give a sense of what the Indian cultures brought to western settlement, I draw portraits of three remarkable North American tribes—the Iroquois, who, though not western themselves, fostered democratic concepts that influenced the framers of the Constitution of the United States; the Cherokees, who created a new homeland in Oklahoma after being uprooted from their communities in Georgia; and the Pueblo Indians of the Southwest, who built a remarkably peaceful, stable society based on religious teachings that emphasized order, moderation, and unanimity.

The Trekkers

To give European settlement in the Old West a human face, chapter 2 sketches the lives of a set of pioneering families. They happen to be my great-grandparents and two great-grandparents of my wife, Lee. Like other Trekker families who crossed the Great Plains, these men and women were of Abraham Lincoln's generation, born in the first decades of the nineteenth century. These ancestors, Mormons all, were no more virtuous, brave, or resourceful than other pioneers who immigrated to the Far West on wagon roads. However, they left extensive journals and memoirs indicating common experiences of the frontier folk who struggled to adapt to unfamiliar, often hostile environments.

The stories of these Trekkers reveal the premium such families put on building communities and the inordinate energy they devoted to completing irrigation systems, bridges, churches, and other projects that would ensure a better life for their children.

This was a daunting undertaking, for at the outset, westering families had to make do with whatever shovels, picks, axes, plows, trowels, chisels, knives, hunting rifles, needles, and spinning wheels they were able to load into their wagons.

Explorers, Fur Trappers, and Settlement

The history of western settlement has been warped by interpreters whose dramatic portraits of explorers and other transient outriders have, too often, diminished the importance of the community-building work of settlers who came to stay. Classic exploration involves the gathering of basic information about a new, unknown geographic area. In what became the United States, the discoveries made by military expeditions, led by such men as Meriwether Lewis and William Clark, Zebulon Pike, Stephen Long, and John Charles Frémont, certainly helped prepare the way for westward expansion.

Because adventures into new country are exciting, the significance of explorers' deeds—and the insights itinerant fur trappers passed on about western terrain—often have been overdrawn in accounts of U.S. history, even to the detriment of the observations of other explorers. This mistake can be seen in Americanized versions of events that distort the far-flung, diverse nature of western exploration itself. For example, Alexander Mackenzie of Great Britain crossed the Rocky Mountains in 1793 and reached the Pacific Ocean thirteen years before Lewis and Clark appeared at the mouth of the Columbia River, yet he is rarely mentioned in standard histories. And in 1541, three centuries before the Southwest region was rediscovered by U.S. citizens, a large party led by Spain's Francisco Vásquez de Coronado explored an area stretching from western California to the Grand Canyon and on to the Smoky Hill River in Kansas, but this is seldom acknowledged. Finally, a huge swath of the Great Basin (supposedly discovered by the "great pathfinder" Frémont in 1843) was traversed and mapped in 1776 by a party led by Franciscan friars from Santa Fe who were sent to locate an overland trail to Monterrey, Mexico.

No one has done more to belittle the accomplishments of the wagon settlers than the late Bernard De Voto, whose work is the subject of chapter 3. De Voto was a superlative writer, but he stretched history when he portrayed the crude, mostly illiterate beaver trappers who roamed parts of the Rocky Mountains as "conquerors" who somehow "bequeathed" a tamed West to the families who came to the region to build homes and communities. In his zeal to glorify the beaver-hunters, De Voto failed to acknowledge that itinerant trappers were not settlers, that military officers on reconnaissance missions were not settlers, and that frenzied single men hell-bent on searching for gold and then returning home were not settlers.

Bernard De Voto was not content to put his trappers on a pinnacle of history. He scoffed at the cultures of native peoples, denigrated the monumental settlement work of the immigrants and missionaries, and even pontificated that Americans who went west were inspired by a pseudo-religion called Manifest Destiny.

The Pivotal Role of Religion

An overarching but neglected truth about the settlement of the American West is that, in the crucial early stages, it was the work of groups animated by religious beliefs. This is the subject of chapter 4. From the first Spanish Catholic colonists arriving in present-day New Mexico in 1598 to the waves of westbound caravans crossing the Rocky Mountains before the gold rush of 1849, people of faith were in the vanguard of western settlement.

Unfortunately, the role of religion in early settlement has been pushed aside by modern historians whose outlook is influ-

enced by what Stephen L. Carter called a "culture of disbelief."
These savants' misjudgments can be linked to a failure to appreciate the powerful influence exerted on the lives of American Protestants in the first half of the nineteenth century by the upsurge of faith and personal commitment known as the Second Great Awakening.

To understand the impetus that brought the first settlers to the Oregon Country, for example, one must first understand the fervor generated by this spiritual awakening. In his authoritative *Religious History of the American People,* Sydney Ahlstrom describes the "immense evangelical energy loosed in New England and America" by that social phenomenon and traces it to the widespread development of home and foreign missionary societies and religious voluntary associations.

Historians who are inclined to discount the influence of religion on American life and politics should reevaluate some of their assumptions. The anti-slavery agitation that led to the Civil War and the emancipation of African Americans was, in large measure, the work of Protestant ministers and members of their congregations. Moreover, contemporary scholars of the American Revolution, such as the late Alan Heimert of Harvard University, have concluded that the key to the majestic insubordination that produced the Declaration of Independence was the "protesting" spirit nurtured by Puritan thought and the teachings of Protestant churches. In the story of western settlement, that spirit, too, deserves a place of honor.

The Illusive Doctrine of Manifest Destiny

Although overland migration was well under way before demagogues in Washington began popularizing the chauvinistic slogan "Manifest Destiny," this concept was later exalted as the motive that inspired westering before the California gold rush.

But one searches in vain in the writings of Oregon-bound Protestants, Mormons, or earlier overland migrants to California for convincing evidence that these groups considered themselves "agents of empire" for the young country they had departed.

Manifest Destiny has been evoked in support of gross misinterpretations of the history of an epoch—just as it has stained the nineteenth-century story of the American advance. In truth, this doctrine slouches along in the march of history alongside such shibboleths as the Divine Right of Kings, the White Man's Burden (a catchphrase flourished by defenders of the British Empire to justify its dominion over other peoples), and the consoling sermons delivered by Christian clerics in the Old South that made slave owners executors of the Lord's Will.

Chapter 5 represents an effort to puncture the Manifest Destiny balloon and remind us that this pernicious political "doctrine" contravened the cardinal principles set forth in the Declaration of Independence. Whether used to justify the greedy culture of gold miners, to condone the flagrant injustices inflicted on native peoples, or to transform single-minded wagon pioneers into flag-waving supporters of imperialistic aims, this deceptive slogan is, first and last, a betrayal of the best American ideals.

The California Gold Rush and Change in the West

No event in United States history has evoked more exaggerations and myths than the human stampede known as the California gold rush. Beginning with Bret Harte, its chroniclers have depicted it as a fountainhead of the American dream, a symbol of the daring that enabled young Americans to conquer the frontier, and a fast-moving development that "opened" the West and changed its history.

Such extravagant interpretation turned western history on its head. It is outlandish to picture the frenetic single men who

arrived in northern California in 1849 as frontline founders of a
frontier civilization. Settlement in the Far West became a reality when the Whitman and Spalding families proved that travel
in wagons from St. Louis to Oregon was feasible—thirteen
years *before* the California rush. By the time the single-minded
gold seekers reached their destinations, the crucial groundbreaking phase of overland migration had already been completed.

The California gold rush did influence events in some parts of
the West. And it had a dark underside that is usually given short
shrift by its chroniclers. Chapter 6 evaluates the overall effects of
the gold rush and puts them in a West-wide perspective from
which the contributions made by San Francisco's capitalists can
be acknowledged along with such negative legacies as virulent
anti-Asian racism and destructive land-use practices that subsequently caused problems in other parts of the West.

Bootstrap Capitalism

In his book *Colony and Empire: The Capitalist Transformation of
the American West,* economic historian William G. Robbins
makes the sweeping claim that capital investments by the
Guggenheim, Gould, Harriman, Hearst, Morgan, and Mellon
families determined the course of development in the West. It is
true that, beginning about 1880, outside capitalists made investments that ultimately ushered the West into the mainstream of
the industrial age. However, such contentions are mischievous if
they convey an impression that the pre-1880 West was inhabited
by horse-and-buggy folk who were passively waiting for captains
of the Gilded Age to bring modern machines into their midst.
The Old West was not a primitive outback. As soon as communities were established, settlers began casting about for economic
opportunities and pooling resources to start ventures that might

be called bootstrap capitalism. These local efforts evolved into companies that put steamships on some rivers and heavy freight wagons on roads that led to evanescent mining camps or incipient centers of trade and commerce.

Indigenous western capitalists such as George Hearst, Collis P. Huntington, and their friends founded vital pioneering enterprises in the region years before the appearance of the fortune-seeking Goulds and Guggenheims and their ilk. The economic takeoff Robbins described did not occur overnight; in large measure, its success was ensured by the impressive infrastructure the settlers created. It was the homes they built, the canals they dug, the orchards they planted, the fields they plowed—and the communities, colleges, and political institutions they established—that laid vital foundations for the city building and industrial development that flowered after the railways arrived.

The Mythology of Western Violence

Mythmakers have depicted the early American West as an unstable region riven by conflicts resolved by gunplay. The misconceptions wrapped around this theme owe their existence to a century-long stream of "western" films and pulp novels. The influence of these fictions is attested by the fact that a standard dictionary (*American Heritage*) contains this definition: "Wild West. The western United States during the period of its settlement, especially with reference to its lawlessness."

William Kittredge has called films "the imperial art of our culture," and today's history teachers begin their labors aware that their students' views of western settlement have been gleaned from film and television screenings. The settlers' West faded into the shadows as the world created by filmmakers gained credence. The transforming power of celluloid mythmakers was recently certified when movie historian Jack Kroll pronounced that "the

Western movie along with jazz is America's foremost indigenous cultural contribution."

Historian Richard Slotkin carved out a niche for himself not by studying the West of the settlers but by focusing on the alchemy by which artists transformed stories of western history into myths that influenced the everyday thinking of Americans. Slotkin was interested not so much in frontier facts as in the effect of western films on American life, thought, and politics. As a pioneer in the new field of cultural history, Slotkin viewed western films as a cultural mechanism that produced a "system of value and meaning" by which people interpreted the world and their lives.

Slotkin concluded that violence in western films had helped to create a macho culture in the United States, and he summarized his findings in a 1992 book, *Gunfighter Nation: The Myth of the Frontier in Twentieth-Century America.* The grand theme of his work is that popular belief in the Wild West fables has caused them to take on the appearance of facts, a rubric that owes a debt to Robert Frost's mischievous dictum that sometimes what is called history is actually gossip.

A senior western historian, Richard Maxwell Brown, put embroidery on Slotkin's thesis by writing tomes asserting that violence was "a principal factor" in the shaping of the West's civilization. Under his magnifying glass, every land dispute between ranchers or conflict between workers and employers that involved gunplay was classified as a "war." Even though the so-called wars he assiduously documents were short-lived, Brown presents them as seminal events of western settlement.

In the first part of chapter 9, I trace the origins of Wild West myths and challenge interpretations that I believe have warped the authentic story of western settlement. In the second part of the chapter, I use the time window of 1878–1881 to demonstrate how insignificant the glorified gunfights of Billy the Kid and Wyatt Earp were to the peaceful, civilizing work their contemporaries were performing in New Mexico and Arizona.

In short, this book asks the reader to rethink the West and its history by bringing into focus the lives and bedrock achievements of the wagon settlers. Whether they emigrated from Mexico in the sixteenth century or from other venues in the nineteenth, these pioneers did not think of themselves as heroes. Collectively, however, they laid foundations that enabled their progeny and their region to become a vibrant part of the world at the dawn of the twenty-first century.

I | Beginnings

1 Native Peoples: The First Forgotten Founders

"The Indians, in the little which they have done, have unquestionably displayed as much natural genius as peoples of Europe in their greatest undertakings."
—Alexis de Tocqueville

*A*merica's truly *first* settlers were, of course, native inhabitants, not just in the West but also in the East. Much of what various Indian groups did has disappeared from history as they were displaced, killed off, or confined by the encroaching Europeans. Even so, native peoples developed some settlements that have persisted to the present day. And evidence indicates that their influence on the patterns and success of European settlement, even on some of its institutions, though often belittled or ignored, was substantial. The first colonists who landed in Massachusetts and Virginia in the sixteenth century, for example, survived harsh winters because their Indian hosts shared the grains and foodstuffs they had stored. The history of the *Mayflower* Pilgrims suggests that the natives in the vicinity of Plymouth Rock not only provided fresh food but also taught the newcomers to raise corn and to fertilize their gardens with alewives harvested in nearby tidal creeks. A similar pageant of salvation took place nearly a century earlier, when Francisco Vásquez de Coronado's starving 1,000-man expedition entered the American Southwest and was fed lifesaving corn that thrifty Pueblo Indian farmers had stored in large granaries.

Although native peoples have conventionally been relegated to the margins of settlement accounts, they are woven deep into the fabric of American history. European settlement of both the East and the West would have been different indeed if Indians had not been there to begin with. Early interactions between Indians and invading Europeans in the Southwest and then, quite independently, in the East set many of the patterns that would be carried over to later encounters in the American West. The first extensive contacts between Europeans and Indians occurred between 1539 and 1542 when two separate Spanish exploring parties, one led by Hernando de Soto and the other by Coronado, conducted far-ranging inland investigations that stretched from Florida north to the Carolinas, along the Mississippi River, into Arkansas, and through eastern California. The treks gave these Europeans an initial look at the geography of the southern sector of what is now the United States and made it possible for them to bring back knowledge about the primitive—and not-so-primitive—societies the aboriginal peoples who populated this region had developed.

Some of the natives encountered by the exploring parties were nomadic, but others lived a pastoral life in villages, hunting game and harvesting a wide variety of crops. Some, the explorers noticed, such as the Pueblo Indians in the Southwest, lived in cohesive communities centered on religious rituals and beliefs. In these communities, native craftsmen erected durable houses and farmers grew grains, fruits, and other crops, practices that yielded living conditions comparable to those of many people in western Europe.

The story of East Coast colonization, at least as presented by the incoming Europeans, can be divided into two distinct phases of interaction with native peoples. The first phase is a positive account of Indians who were peaceful and helpful—the names of Squanto and Pocahontas come up routinely. The second phase is dominated by stories of warriors who refused to submit to the colonists' demands and were driven from their homelands. In Virginia, for example, the peaceful initial period was short-lived because Captain John Smith organized armed food raids. A swashbuckler who viewed the natives as savages who had no rights, Smith pursued an Indian policy that produced unrelenting conflict and that, within forty years of Jamestown's founding, left the remnants of the once-powerful Powhatan Indians scrambling to eke out a living on the fringes of the region the tribe once had dominated.

In New England, the initial phase of European settlement followed a somewhat different path largely because the colonists there were refugees who had experienced religious persecution, and they put a premium on personal freedom and peace. The outlook that governed the first decades of Puritan settlement— and helped produce a "treaty" of peace with the Wampanoag Indians that lasted forty years—was articulated in these directives issued by the officers of the Massachusetts Bay Company:

> Above all, we pray you to be careful that there be none in our precincts permitted to do any injury, in the least kind, to the heathen people [and] if any of the savages pretend right of inheritance to all or any part of the lands granted in our patent, we pray you endeavor to purchase their title.

No New England leader did more to fulfill the letter and the spirit of these injunctions than Roger Williams. A fiery advocate of religious freedom, Williams was a friend of poet John Milton and had known Oliver Cromwell. On being banished from Massachusetts in 1635, he founded Providence, the first settlement of Rhode Island, as a haven for Quakers and other dissenters. He subsequently won the trust of Narragansett Indians by treating them as equals and by insisting that they be paid for title to their land.

But such endeavors came to naught as the flow of immigrants into southern New England swelled and the desire for Indian lands became more compelling than the commitment to maintain good relations. The Puritan perspective soon changed to accommodate the new situation, and native homelands were seized on the pretext that "civilized" men had a God-given right to displace a culture deemed inferior. Welcome of the peace that had prevailed for three decades was replaced among Puritans by a conviction that there was an unbridgeable gulf between the two societies. This hubris in turn extinguished earlier hopes that a policy of tolerance would allow Puritans and natives to live harmoniously in the same valleys.

The hopelessness and despair these events generated in the minds of New England's natives led to a bloody uprising in 1675. The year-long, region-wide conflict (misnamed King Philip's War by the Puritans) had tragic consequences for both sides. The casualties were severe. When the killing ended, all hopes for peace were extinguished and the scattered natives of southern New England were left landless.

Historians who argue that such an outcome was inevitable have failed to reckon with the contrasting peace policy initiated six years later along the Delaware River by Quaker proprietor William Penn. By the time of Penn's first visit to his new colony in 1682, he had already made history in England by writings and speeches that distinguished him as a fearless advocate for religious tolerance. In Pennsylvania he put flesh on his words by making the colony a haven for Mennonites, Amish, Dunkers,

Moravians, and members of other religious sects suffering persecution in Europe.

A friendly Indian policy was the centerpiece of the "holy experiment" in democracy Penn sponsored with his Society of Friends. In negotiating to purchase land from the Delaware Indians, Penn informed them, "I desire to enjoy it with your consent, that we may always live together as neighbors and friends." His handpicked Quaker successors made fair dealing a cornerstone of public life, providing a foundation of mutual respect that enabled Penn's colony to avoid Indian hostilities for eighty years.

This history is informative. However, we can gain a more intimate sense of the varied and important contributions of native groups to American settlement if we look at three Indian tribes—the Iroquois, the Cherokees, and the Pueblos—each located progressively farther west geographically and each with quite different fates in their encounters with the Europeans and their descendants who crossed the sea.

The Iroquois

In the eighteenth century, the Iroquois League—known to the British as the Six Nations—was among the most impressive indigenous civilizations in the Americas. The homeland of these tribes stretched across what is now upstate New York from Amsterdam to Rochester, in effect forming a buffer zone between British and French settlements in the lower Great Lakes region. The cohesion of their confederacy conferred power, and the skills the Iroquois mastered as town builders, farmers, hunters, and warriors made them a force to be feared and respected.

Governed by a council that operated by consensus, each well-kept village was a self-sustaining unit. Bark-covered longhouses more than 100 feet in length provided shelter for ten to twelve families, and the surrounding farms and orchards furnished a variety of foods. In season, the natives of the Six Nations ranged widely and excelled as hunters, fishermen, traders, and fur trappers.

In the 1750s, as the British and French vied for military dominance in the area, both sides sought to forge alliances with tribes who could augment the strength of their modest armies. After a French force that included only 254 regular soldiers but 600 Ottawa Indians decimated General Edward Braddock's army near present-day Pittsburgh in July 1755, the British redoubled their efforts to win over native tribes that lived along the route of likely French encroachments.

Two "Indian superintendents" were appointed to implement this strategy. William Johnson, who had maintained a trading post in the Mohawk Valley for many years, was chosen to represent England's interests in the north country. Edmond Atkin was selected to fulfill this function on the southward frontier. While the bulk of the colonists along the Atlantic seaboard took stock in the myth that the Indians they had driven out were cruel and subhuman, Atkin discovered that British officials engaged in face-to-face dealings with backcountry natives had a high regard for their qualities, and he came to share these views:

> No people in the world understand and pursue their true national interests better than the Indians. [H]ow sanguinary so ever they are towards their enemies, from a misguided passion of heroism, and a love of their country; yet they are in other ways truly humane, hospitable and equitable. . . . In their public treaties, no people on earth are more open, explicit, and direct, nor are they excelled by any in the observance of them.

Johnson, a staunch Tory, won the trust and friendship of the Iroquois by deeds. His estate was a center of Indian trade and a shelter for Mohawk people. His wife was a Mohawk, and his understanding of Indian values encouraged natives to let him mediate their disputes. Historians give Johnson credit for serving England's interests by keeping the Iroquois neutral during the war with the French that ended in 1763.

The tragic destruction of the Six Nations came about when the League's neutrality policy was ignored and outside pressures sucked the Iroquois into the vortex of the military struggle known as the American Revolution. Having no visible stake in the outcome, the confederation's Grand Council wisely voted in 1776 not to take sides in the conflict. However, Joseph Brant, a charismatic Mohawk who had recently returned from England, defied the authority of the Council and launched an impassioned campaign to recruit natives to serve as attack soldiers for the Crown. It would be the undoing of the Iroquois.

For all practical purposes, Brant was a British agent. Schooled at Dartmouth College and in England, he had served as an official in the Tory government. The arguments he used to enlist Iroquois warriors were, in effect, those of a British patriot's war speech. And the wedge Brant drove divided the Six Nations. The Oneidas and the Tuscaroras sided with George Washington's armies while Mohawk and Cayuga warriors, led by Brant and equipped by British officers, conducted scorched earth raids against forts and settlements on the New York frontier.

Brant's bloody victories provoked a draconian response in 1779 when General George Washington sent a 3,000-man army to burn Iroquois villages and destroy their crops. Even the soldiers sent to carry out this pitiless mission were impressed with the civilization these natives had built over a period of two centuries. "The Indians live much better than most of the Mohawk Valley farmers," one wrote, "their houses very well furnished with all of the necessary household utensils, great plenty of grain, several horses, cows and waggons." The 1779 raid ended the dominance of the Six Nations in their upstate New York homeland. A diaspora followed that saw vanquished Iroquois fleeing to Canada and as far away as Wisconsin while a remnant population was allowed to remain in restricted enclaves.

Even though their culture was decimated, the Six Nations played a vital role in U.S. constitutional history. In formulating its charter, the fledgling United States of America had no European precedent to follow. However, leaders such as Benjamin Franklin, Thomas Paine, Charles Thompson, and Thomas Jefferson were impressed by the structure of the Iroquois confederacy, and it was on their minds when they devised a constitution based on principles of federalism.

The Iroquois League left another legacy as well—the concept of tribal sovereignty, which became the Magna Carta for native people in the United States. From the beginning, British administrators acknowledged the self-governance of the Iroquois and other tribes and conducted relations with them as separate governments through formal treaties. The Iroquois culture symbolized the reality that Indian groups had the capacity to govern their internal affairs.

After the Revolution, the new nation continued the practice of recognizing tribes as sovereign governments, and the United States Supreme Court, in a magisterial opinion written in 1832 by Chief Justice John Marshall, put a constitutional cloak over tribal sovereignty and the rights of native peoples. Citing "the settled doctrine of the law of nations," Justice Marshall declared that "the Indian nations [of the United States] had always been considered as distinct, independent political communities, retaining their original natural rights." Thus, though the Six Nations lost most of their land, one brilliant concept of governance they developed continues to burn brightly even today.

The Cherokees

Two decades after the Iroquois tragedy drew to a close, in the mountains of northern Georgia the Cherokee Indians were engaged in a remarkable process of cultural self-transformation. The process commenced in 1801 when Moravian missionaries convinced the Cherokees that their chances of retaining their homelands would be improved if they made adaptations white men had to respect.

The Cherokees took up this challenge, and in just one generation they made revolutionary advances. Their Moravian friends convinced them that an important emblem of respectability was a written language. In short order, a gifted young Cherokee, Sequoya (a soldier who had fought in one of Andrew Jackson's armies), invented a syllabary alphabet for the Cherokee language, which was soon mastered by the entire tribe. The Cherokees celebrated this newly won literacy with another accomplishment: publication of a newspaper, the *Cherokee Phoenix*.

The creative achievements of the Cherokees were substantial in many technological and material spheres as well. An 1826 report to the congregation of the First Presbyterian Church in Philadelphia presented this summary of their efforts:

> At this time there are 22,000 cattle, 7,600 horses, 46,000 swine, 2,500 sheep, 762 looms, 1,400 spinning wheels, 172 wagons, 2,048 plows, 10 saw mills, 31 grist mills, 62 blacksmith shops, 8 cotton machines, 18 schools, 18 ferries . . . and [a library] with upward of 1,000 volumes of good books.

In addition to these developments, the Cherokees approved a written constitution, developed a republican form of government, and chose John Ross as their principal chief. Of mixed ancestry and tutored by the missionaries, Ross fit the Georgia mold: a proprietor of successful businesses, he owned a large plantation and slaves and dressed like a southern planter. Had Georgia's political leaders been open-minded, they would have realized that the Cherokees had the potential to contribute more to the general welfare than most of the semi-literate Europeans who were immigrating to that state.

The Cherokees desperately needed a leader of Ross' caliber when Andrew Jackson, a sworn enemy of Indian claims to land, was elected president in 1828. A former lawyer and land speculator on the frontier, Jackson viewed treaties with the Indians as "an absurdity not to be reconciled with the principles of our government." He favored an apartheid solution to the "Indian question" that involved the removal of all natives to a wilderness somewhere beyond the Mississippi River. This scheme became national policy when the United States Congress passed Jackson's Indian Removal Act in 1830.

John Ross mounted a forceful campaign to soften the views of the nation's leaders. He, too, had served as a soldier under General Jackson, and he made frequent trips to Washington, D.C., during which he presented appeals for justice to the president and members of Congress. When President Jackson refused to listen and the state of Georgia passed a law seizing the Cherokee homeland, Ross and his friends, as a last resort, filed cases with the Supreme Court. These lawsuits set a precedent by raising seminal legal issues regarding Indian rights. In a great victory for the Cherokees and other Indian tribes, Chief Justice John Marshall ruled that Georgia's landgrab violated the Constitution and laws of the United States.

This decision was turned to ashes, however, when an obdurate president flouted the nation's Constitution. In a startling display of contempt for the Supreme Court—and for the rights of American Indians—President Jackson scoffed at the Court's decision. With a nod to his Georgia friends, he quipped, "[Marshall] has rendered his decision, now let him enforce it." Ignoring the oath he had taken to uphold the Constitution, Jackson advised Georgia's officials to use terror tactics to win what they had lost in the courts of law. "Build a fire under them," he counseled. "When it gets hot enough, they'll move."

For eight years the Cherokees refused to abandon their homes, but ultimately Congress fixed a deadline, and in 1838 President Martin Van Buren, Jackson's handpicked successor, sent an army of 7,000 soldiers to remove the Cherokees to a region of the far frontier where the Choctaws, Chickasaws, and Creeks had already been "relocated." The outcome was the infamous 1,000-mile forced march the Cherokees called the Trail of Tears. Ross obtained a concession from the commanding general to organize his nation of 18,000 refugees into thirteen groups for the journey. This strategy saved thousands of lives, but more than 4,000 Cherokees, including Ross' wife, perished.

Andrew Jackson did more to subvert the cause of Indian justice than any other president of the United States. His "final solution" had disastrous consequences for the country's native inhabitants. By turning indigenous peoples into outcasts, his policy denied many, many thousands the opportunity to make valuable social and cultural contributions to American life.

Jackson's policies cast a prolonged, baleful influence on American attitudes and Indian policy making. They fostered the myth that Indians were savages who could not be civilized. They legitimized the concept that Indian treaties could—and should—be broken with impunity. And they implanted the idea in Washington that so-called Indian problems ultimately had to be resolved by military force. This corrosive conviction influenced the decision of the nation's leaders to send troops into the West after the Civil War to subjugate the Indians and to provoke the one-sided skirmishes they called "Indian wars."

In 1881, the Episcopal bishop of Minnesota, H. B. Whipple, aptly described the harm Andrew Jackson's policies had done to the national ethic. "The American people," the bishop observed, "have accepted as truth the teaching that the Indians were a degraded, brutal race of savages who it was the will of God should perish at the approach of civilization."

The Pueblo Indians

During an 1830 debate in the United States Senate about President Jackson's Indian removal legislation, Senator Theodore Frelinghuysen of New Jersey raised moral questions the advocates of this scheme had ignored. "I believe, sir," he proclaimed,

> it is not now seriously denied that the Indians are men, endowed with kindred faculties and powers with ourselves. In the light of natural law, can a reason for a distinction exist in the mode of enjoying [land] which [one owns]? Is it one of the prerogatives of the white man that he may disregard the dictates of moral principles when an Indian is concerned?

Had this debate taken place two decades later, the senator might have cited the Pueblo Indians in the newly annexed New Mexico Territory to support his contention that removal was a misguided policy. There, Frelinghuysen might have argued, was living proof that Europeans and natives not only could coexist in the same valley but also could interact in ways that benefited both cultures.

In 1540, when soldiers of Coronado's exploring expedition climbed onto the high deserts of the Colorado Plateau, they encountered not another Aztec empire but a more advanced civilization, the members of which they named the Pueblo (town) Indians. In observing the culture and lifestyle of these aborigines, the Spaniards found many things to admire. At Zuni, they remarked on the construction techniques local masons used to build rugged, multi-storied communal dwellings. They were fascinated by the ingenious methods the farmers used to cultivate thousands of acres of lowlands with the floodwaters from infrequent rains. But most of all, the European invaders were impressed by the orderliness and cohesion of Pueblo culture. In a letter to the king of Spain, Coronado reported that the Zunis were highly intelligent, and he praised their dignity and the discipline that governed their lives. His scribe, Pedro de Castañeda, added these words to describe their religion and the social behavior it inculcated:

> They do not have chiefs as in New Spain [Mexico] but are ruled by a council of the oldest men. They have priests who . . . go up on the highest roof of the village and preach to the village from there, like public criers, in the morning when the sun is rising, the whole village being silent and sitting in the galleries to listen. They tell them how to live, and I believe they give certain commandments for them to keep, for there is no drunkenness among them, nor sodomy or sacrifices, neither do they eat flesh nor steal, but they are usually at work.

This admiration would have widened had the Spaniards stayed long enough to learn how the religion of these natives was interwoven with everyday life and seasonal rituals. The conduct of the Pueblo Indians was well ordered because their religion held that personal fulfillment would come through family unity and communal happiness. They abhorred Aztecan displays of power or domination by so-called kings or nobles. Harmony was a central theme of their worship, and their ways centered on constant communion with the natural world. The social goals they had distilled from centuries of experience in a lean environment were amity, not conquest; stability, not strife; conservation, not waste; restraint, not aggression.

The ethos that sustained the centuries-old culture of these villages embraced concepts of fellowship and order that produced balanced, peace-seeking communities and preserved a pattern of independent village life. It dampened the combative impulses that pitched so many New World tribes into destructive wars, and it dissuaded villages from seeking dominion over other pueblos or other Indian groups.

The mature Pueblo outlook was an outgrowth of a wise, tenacious civilization developed by ancestors who, five centuries earlier, had created a flourishing culture that radiated outward from a sacred center in western New Mexico's Chaco Canyon. The Chacoans were resourceful farmers in a harsh environment who, about A.D. 900, built a complex of apartments that was one of the largest dwelling structures in the world. Their religious shrines were the surrounding majestic mesas, buttes, and mountains, and their society was based on a conviction that human energy should be used to promote life and to care for the primal needs of people.

The Spanish immigrants who settled first in the land of the Pueblos came into the Rio Grande valley along the southern edge of the Rocky Mountains in 1598, after undertaking an arduous overland journey of nearly 1,000 miles from central Mexico. These settlers consisted of 129 family groups, 10 Franciscan friars, and a contingent of 270 soldiers. In the expedition's caravan were 83 wagons and carts loaded with seeds, seedlings, tools, and household goods; in the vanguard, herdsmen drove 7,000 horses, mules, cattle, sheep, and goats.

In 1610, these immigrants established a capital in Santa Fe and sponsored a mission colony supported by the king of Spain. Although resources supplied from Mexico were meager, this wilderness mission flourished, thanks mainly to the zeal of the Franciscan priests. By 1650, nearly fifty friars had converted thousands of natives to the Catholic faith and established thirty-five missions adjacent to individual pueblos. The missionaries provided each community with animals, orchards, and catechisms, and their converts responded by building churches, schools, convents, and workshops.

Unlike the situation in New England, the bone of contention in this spacious region was not land but religion. From the outset, Pueblo religious leaders resented the proselytizing of the Franciscans and their attempts to undermine the ancient system of worship that had kept Pueblo Indian communities unified. They exercised restraint until the 1670s, when a particularly obtuse and intolerant Spanish governor misjudged their importance and power and launched a violent campaign of persecution against them.

By the time the governor's "purification" program was complete, forty-seven native religious leaders had been accused of sorcery, three shamans had been hanged and others whipped, and performances of native religious rituals had been banned. This was a fateful blunder. The governor was apparently oblivious to the reality that a tacit truce with the Pueblos prevailed only because the native religious leaders had not gone on the attack. He also failed to recognize that the natives outnumbered the Spaniards by ten to one.

The Pueblo Rebellion of 1680 was a whirlwind of terror. The uprising lasted only two weeks, but in the end Santa Fe had been sacked, 21 Franciscan friars and 380 colonists had been killed, churches had been desecrated, and the governor and the survivors were straggling downriver to El Paso.

It took the Spanish twelve years to regroup, but in 1692 a campaign to reestablish Spanish hegemony began. A new governor, Diego de Vargas, traveled with a small, well-disciplined army to several pueblos, informing their leaders that he did not intend to punish those who had carried out the rebellion. Like Hernán Cortés in Mexico, Vargas preferred diplomacy to force. After retaking Santa Fe in a one-day skirmish, he spent several months conducting conciliatory meetings at various pueblos.

Despite his overtures, in the summer of 1696 warriors at a few pueblos killed their new friars and started a new round of fighting. But by now the governor had persuaded five pueblos to join his crusade, and he was able to quell what proved to be the final insurrection.

In the rebellion's aftermath, a tacit live-and-let-live arrangement gradually took hold. There never was a formal peace conference, but during the decades that followed, a spirit of tolerance grew as both sides renewed old patterns of cooperation and realized that mutual benefits would flow if religious strife could be avoided.

From the beginning, the Spanish settlers had been impressed by elements of Pueblo culture that involved building and living with the earth. They copied the adobe construction techniques Pueblo craftsmen had developed and adopted the irrigation practices perfected by Indian farmers to harvest crops of indigenous corn, beans, chilies, and cotton.

The process of adaptation was a two-way street. Thus, the Franciscans not only provided European tools (axes, adzes, spades, hoes, saws) but also set up workshops at their missions to teach Pueblo Indians European styles of weaving, shoemaking, tailoring, carpentry, and smithery. Orchards were planted, and the Pueblos began to use horses, oxen, cows, pigs, and sheep to improve their well-being.

As religious tolerance was fostered in both societies, it produced an ecumenical outcome that was remarkable. Some Pueblo natives became devout Catholics; others remained true to the tenets of their parents. A large middle group kept strong ties to both faiths, embracing elements of Catholicism while continuing to participate in the secret rites and ceremonies of their ancestors. Cooperation acquired a vital new dimension in the middle decades of the eighteenth century when marauding bands of Plains Indians began raiding villages in the Rio Grande valley. The Spaniards and natives responded by organizing joint patrols to improve the security of their towns.

The extraordinary nature of the compromises that led to a triumph of tolerance in this secluded area of North America is all the more remarkable because it took place during a period when most European nations were still embroiled in religious wars and persecutions. The enlightenment embodied in what might be called the New Mexico compromise is equally startling given the policies of Indian dispossession and removal that prevailed elsewhere in what is now the United States.

The settlement of the Southwest was singular in that Europeans made—and kept—agreements concerning the land rights of the Pueblo Indians such that today their descendants live on the same land they occupied before the first explorers set foot on the continent.

The tolerance that produced such an outcome in the Southwest raises questions about the attitudes and motives that generated harsh policies in other regions of the country. Would American history have been more humane, one wonders, if there had been fewer men like Andrew Jackson and more like Roger Williams and William Penn, who, from the outset, viewed natives not as uncouth savages but as fellow human beings? One wonders, too, whether native peoples would have been regarded as inferior if—as in French Canada—substantial numbers of incoming Europeans had cast aside ideas of ethnic purity and married Indian women.

In retrospect, it is painfully clear that innumerable demeaning chapters of American history could have been avoided if more European immigrants had been open-minded about concepts of equality and coexistence.

2 European Settlers: Human Faces, Far-Flung Places

*W*hen Juan de Oñate led his party of Spanish families, Franciscan friars, and soldiers into a valley in what is now northern New Mexico in 1598, an animating purpose of this, the first European settlement of the Old West, was expressly religious. Having some knowledge of the region through Francisco Vásquez de Coronado's earlier explorations, the viceroy in Mexico City wanted to expand the reach of Spain's empire by establishing a missionary colony near the Pueblo Indian homeland.

Spain lacked the resources to achieve martial conquests in its political domain, and for the next two centuries it pursued a plan favored by prelates in Rome: expand the rim of Christendom by proselytizing. In what became the United States, one strand of this effort culminated in the founding of Tucson in 1776 and erection of the splendid Mission San Xavier del Bac to serve nearby native peoples. Later strands of this campaign included the establishment of missions and frontier communities in eastern

Western Settlement
by
Religious Groups,
1598–1857

Missions begun by
Pierre-Jean De Smet
and the Jesuits,
1841–1846

Settlements established
in the Oregon Country by
Protestant missionaries,
1834–ca. 1855

Areas settled
by Mormon
colonists,
1847–1857

Area of
Catholic
missions
and settlements,
1769–1820

Franciscan missions
and Spanish settlements,
1598–1820

Areas where Catholic
missions and settlements
were initiated by Spain,
1681–1820

Area missionized and
explored by Eusebio Kino
and his successors,
ca. 1700–1820

Walla
Walla
Lapwai
Bitterroot
Valley
Lemhi
Salmon R.
Snake
River
Columbia R.
Willamette Vly.
Missouri River
Platte River
OREGON TRAIL
OREGON TRAIL
Kansas City
Missouri
River
Carson
Valley
CALIFORNIA TRAIL
Salt Lake City
River
Moab
Colorado
Sacramento
Hopi
Pueblos
San Juan
Taos
Santa Fe
Pecos
Rio Grande
Arkansas River
Red River
San Bernardino
San Diego
Gila
River
Tucson
El Paso
Rio Grande
Chihuahua
EL CAMINO REAL
San Saba
San Antonio
Goliad
Laredo
Nacogdoches
PACIFIC
OCEAN
GULF OF MEXICO
TO MEXICO CITY

N

SCALE IN MILES
0   250   500

Reade

Texas (mainly in the period 1681–1820) and creation of a string of missions in the California coastlands between 1769 and 1820, guided by Father Junípero Serra and his followers.

The impetus for much of the early European settlement of the West more generally came from the churches, but not just Catholic ones. First indeed were the Catholic orders, mainly in the Southwest and the Far West, though also, much later, in the Montana region. Western settlement inspired by Protestantism was extensive, too, as we'll see in chapter 4, most notably among those who traveled overland on the Oregon Trail and settled in the Oregon Country from 1834 to about 1855. (See the Western Settlement map.) And later still, with a high tide in the period 1847–1857, were the Mormons, who sought sanctuary in Spain's Great Basin region.

If the inspiration for these early settlers was often divine, their desires were eminently social and practical as well. These were sojourners who worked hard to establish new homes and communities, not simply people who showed up to exploit resources and then return home. They went to extraordinary lengths and sacrificed much to travel so far, establish themselves in the West, and build communities there. To faith we have to add fortitude. A shortcoming of histories that concentrate on broad outlines of events is the absence of human faces and stories of ordinary folk that would reveal what animated individuals and families and indicate the experiences they had. Yet only by considering individual human experience can we begin to develop a sense of what these men and women faced and an idea of the magnitude of their achievements.

To overcome this deficit to some extent, I have, with misgivings, elected to illustrate aspects of early western development, especially the great period of wagon settlers in the 1840s and 1850s, by presenting cameo portraits of great-grandparents who were, in some ways, representative pioneers of that period. I do not pretend that these men and women were more virtuous or brave or resourceful than other westering colonists. They were all of the Mormon faith, only one of the religious persuasions that developed the Old West. But many other attributes—from fortitude in the face of adversity to the capacity and will to fashion a self-sustaining life and develop a stable, moral community—were widely shared among westering immigrants of all religious backgrounds.

Edward Milo Webb (b. 1815) and Amelia Owens Webb (b. 1800s)

The short life of Edward Milo Webb (paternal great-grandfather of my wife, Lee) tracks the early history of the Church of Jesus Christ of Latter-day Saints, or Mormon Church, and its move west. Edward was born in Chautauqua County, New York, in 1815. He and his parents and two brothers were converted to Mormonism in 1834 and moved to Kirtland, Ohio (now a Cleveland suburb). There, together with other members of his newfound faith, Edward helped construct the first Mormon temple. Economic turbulence during the Panic of 1837 caused a schism in the church, and Joseph Smith and his adherents were forced to flee. In a caravan of covered wagons, the Webb family followed their new prophet on a 900-mile trek to a troubled colony in western Missouri called the "new Zion."

By the time the Webbs arrived there in the summer of 1838, mobs had driven Mormons living in the region from their homes, and more than 15,000 of them were cowering in tents and rough-hewn structures north of the Missouri River. The "Missouri drivings" that followed were animated by fear and suspicion. The aggressive proselytizing of Mormon preachers who proclaimed their religion as the only true church outraged local ministers. Politicians saw the sudden influx of thousands of cohesive, zealous settlers as a threat to their power. And slaveholders—Missouri had been admitted to the Union in 1820 as a slave state—viewed these newcomers from free states as prospective abolitionists.

Ignited by a leave-or-be-exterminated order signed by Missouri's governor, these pillars of local opposition created a bonfire of hate that engulfed the Mormon settlers. Widespread beatings and looting, the arrest of Joseph Smith and four other Mormon leaders, and a massacre of seventeen men at Haun's Mill ensued in the fall of 1838. Families were forced to leave behind everything they could not load on a wagon or handcart.

Exhausted and impoverished, some desperate Missouri Mormons made peace with their neighbors, abandoned their church, and kept their farms. The Webbs, however, joined the dispirited, ill-provisioned, and poverty-stricken main caravan making its way to Quincy, Illinois. They lived there for a few weeks and then moved to nearby Payson, Illinois, where Edward and his older brother Chauncy, a wheelwright, went into business as wagonmakers. It was during this period that Edward married Amelia Owens, the daughter of pioneers who had first joined the Mormon Church in Ohio.

Mormon fortunes, both economic and spiritual, reached a nadir in the spring of 1839. The church Smith had founded owned no tangible property, and the condition of his followers, scrambling to survive in the lowlands of the Mississippi River, was pitiable. Even when Smith's jailers allowed him to escape, the outlook remained grim, but Smith was able to revive the spirits of his followers the next summer by locating a new place of settlement.

There seemed little to recommend the spot he chose, a swampy tract of land on the Illinois side of a horseshoe bend in the Mississippi River. But Smith gave two farmers a promissory note for the land and promptly laid out a plan for a model community, which he named Nauvoo, the City Beautiful. Within weeks, his followers were busy draining swamps and planting crops, and on this site in five years indefatigable Mormon exiles built the largest city in the state of Illinois.

Edward Milo Webb worked hard to make the vision of his spiritual leader a reality. He erected a home for his wife and two children in Nauvoo, worked as a carpenter on the new temple, served as a part-time soldier in Smith's Nauvoo Legion, and responded to calls from Smith to evangelize in nearby states.

As the self-styled Saints thrived and Nauvoo swelled with new converts, the church aroused a fresh wave of animosity whipped up by rumors that some of the Mormons, under Joseph Smith's tutelage, were practicing polygamy. This hostility reached a crest in the summer of 1844, when a mob assassinated Smith and Illinois officials demanded that the Saints leave Nauvoo. In the fall of the following year, the governor of Illinois led a crusade to remove Mormons entirely from his state.

Smith's successor, Brigham Young, realized that his sect was unlikely to find lasting peace unless they left the United States and established a homeland somewhere in the Rocky Mountains. In the face of new threats, Young and his followers made a midwinter flight. Temperatures were so low that for an interval in February a mile-long bridge of ice formed on the Mississippi strong enough to sustain heavily loaded wagons. By the first of March, more than 5,000 exiles were hovering around bonfires in temporary wagon camps in the bleak lower bottomlands. To ensure discipline and equitable distribution of food supplies, Young organized the emigrants into traveling units of "Hundreds" and "Fifties" and appointed captains to lead each company.

A move into what he envisioned as a refuge "in the tops of the mountains" would have to be staged over a period of years, Young concluded. A self-sustaining support system had to be created so that the neediest and weakest Saints could make the journey safely. And only with a year's delay in the departure of the first group of settlers would the advance party have enough sturdy wagons to transport the household goods, implements, foodstuffs, and seed grains the emigrants would need in their new land.

Under Young's leadership, crude communities were erected at three staging points in Iowa during the following summer; herds of cattle, sheep, and horses were husbanded; and Mormon farmers produced a crucial surplus of grains to sustain the first wave of emigrants. Young's advance company crossed the Missouri River to a site the Mormons named Winter Quarters (near present-day Omaha), where energetic exiles built 538 log houses and 83 sod houses before the onset of the next winter. Since wagon-making skills were of paramount importance, Chauncy and Edward Webb were included in this vanguard. In April 1847, Brigham Young's exploring party, consisting of 144 men, 3 women, 73 wagons, 93 horses, 52 mules, 66 oxen, and 19 cows, started a 1,000-mile trek into the untrammeled country of the Great Basin. Young rode west in one of Chauncy's wagons, and Mormon lore informs us that when he arrived at a promontory from which the Salt Lake valley could be seen, he halted his team and declared, "This is the place."

Edward Webb delayed emigrating with his family until a caravan left in the summer of 1852. His decision to wait and prepare a strong two-wagon outfit was influenced by the tender ages of his four children and by a desire to migrate with Amelia's relatives. With savings he had accumulated by working as a carpenter and blacksmith, Edward and his family started west with 6 oxen, 2 cows, 24 sheep, and wagons loaded with equipment and a year's provisions.

In late July, as the party moved up the Platte River, an epidemic of acute cholera swept through the wagon train. In three days this fast-moving disease snuffed out the lives of Edward and one of Amelia's relatives. The captain of this Fifty, William Bailey Maxwell, ordered the dead hastily buried, and, in hopes of outrunning the plague, the train moved on.

Dead at age thirty-seven, Edward Milo Webb never saw the Saints' new gathering place. His widow and children mourned on the move, taking comfort in their belief that his passing was the Lord's will. Amelia, grief-stricken and pregnant, held the reins of the front wagon; her nine-year-old son, Marcellus, was placed in charge of the second; and Edward Jr., age five (Lee's grandfather), was given the responsibility of keeping the cows and sheep moving westward alongside the wagons.

A year after Amelia and her children arrived in Salt Lake City, Brigham Young issued a call to her two brothers to help create a community in a southwestern Utah valley later named Fillmore. Amelia joined them, and there she married Alexander MacRae several years later. As a homemaker and community seamstress, Amelia spent her remaining forty years in Fillmore. Like so many strong Mormon women of her era, she dedicated her life to serving her church, to ensuring the welfare of her children, and to building her community in the West.

William Bailey Maxwell (1821–1895) and Lucretia Bracken Maxwell (1823–1893)

Once they reached their Zion-in-the-mountains, most Mormons had the satisfying experience of building homes and living out their lives in the community they helped to settle. However, under Brigham Young's policy of sending selected Saints into the hinterland to establish a network of colonies, men such as William

Bailey Maxwell, another of my wife's ancestors, were assigned roles as movable frontiersmen of the faith. Luckily, Maxwell was a restless individual who welcomed Young's frequent calls to break ground in unsullied valleys. At the end of his days, he held a record of pioneering few could match: he had participated in founding more than thirteen new communities in Utah, Nevada, Arizona, and Mexico (see the W. B. Maxwell map).

A rangy, resourceful individual who cherished new challenges, Maxwell was born in Illinois, moved to Missouri, and by adulthood had become a frontiersman's frontiersman. At nineteen he married a young Mormon woman, Lucretia Bracken, and soon joined her church. Obedient to the commands of their leaders, the Maxwells not only took part in building Joseph Smith's City Beautiful but also managed a church-owned farm and grove of maple-sugar trees across the river in Iowa. In the bitter winter of 1846, they piled their belongings into a wagon and fled with their brethren into Iowa's Indian country.

The following spring found Maxwell joining the U.S. Army. Congress had declared war on Mexico, and President James K. Polk had asked Brigham Young for help in assembling a volunteer army to march west and do battle with Mexican troops in New Mexico and California. With characteristic shrewdness, Young saw an opportunity to kill two birds with one stone: he would court Polk's goodwill by enrolling a cadre of young Mormons (Maxwell among them) in his army—but only after assurances were given that their pay would be funneled into his coffers to help Mormon families equip themselves for the rigors of wilderness travel.

Maxwell left his wife and their two small sons with her father and soon found himself trudging west on the Santa Fe Trail through immense herds of buffalo. After joining up with General Stephen Watts Kearny, the Mormon unit helped occupy Santa Fe

Communities Maxwell helped settle are numbered in sequence from 1 to 13 (1848–1895)

Snake River

Continental

Platte River

OREGON   TRAIL

1847 Maxwell's route home

1847 Maxwell's route home (on horseback)

Council Bluffs

Missouri River

1847 Maxwell's route home (on horseback)

Salt Lake City   Stewart's Ranch

Payson 12

Santaquin 3

Sacramento

Pioche (Springvalley) 6

Panguitch 7

Short Creek 4

Orderville 8

Pipe Spring 5

Moab

Colorado River

1846 Mormon Battalion (walking)

SANTA FE TRAIL

Fort Leavenworth

Arkansas River

San Joaquin R.

(on horseback)

San Bernardino

Taos

Santa Fe

Rio Grande

W. B. Maxwell's Search for New Country and the Thirteen Colonies He Helped to Found

San Diego

1846 Mormon Battalion

Pleasanton

Springerville 9

Alpine 10

11

(walking)

Gila R.

Tucson

El Paso

Quaxco 13

12 Colonia Diaz

Chihuahua

Rio Grande

N

Continental Divide

GULF OF MEXICO

PACIFIC OCEAN

SCALE IN MILES

0   250   500

and then marched southward along the Rio Grande, turned west to a Mexican fort at Tucson, and completed their 2,000-mile march by crossing the Mojave Desert into San Diego.

When these Mormon irregulars were mustered out the following summer, Maxwell and his friends, after months of foot and horse travel, returned to their families in Iowa. But not for long. Bill Maxwell, as we already know, served as captain of a Fifty company when he went west again, this time with his family. He was not allowed to tarry in Salt Lake City when he reached it, however. Brigham Young sent him straight to the southern outpost of Payson, Utah, where he built a house for his family, helped construct a fort where families could gather during Ute Indian raids, and played an important role in helping arrange a peace with the Utes. He was later made a captain when the Utah Militia was mustered to confront the army sent by President James Buchanan in 1857 to quell a supposed Mormon rebellion. Soon thereafter, Maxwell helped establish new communities at Stewart's Ranch and Santaquin.

A larger challenge came in 1862 when Brigham Young told Maxwell to move his family 300 miles south, to the rim of Mormon migration in the Indian country north of the Grand Canyon. With the help of his two eldest sons, Maxwell had become a successful stockman, and he drove his herds to Short Creek, on the Arizona border, where he established a cattle ranch. Again at Young's behest, Maxwell then became the wrangler-manager of a large spread of church-owned cattle in the area surrounding Pipe Spring, Arizona.

In 1866, a new mission call came from Brigham Young. This time, Maxwell was to move his two families to the Utah-Nevada border and help establish settlements near the new silver-mining village of Pioche, Nevada. This was the last, and most felicitous, mission Bill Maxwell would perform for his church. After living for a few months in an adjacent village, he moved a mile north to Springvalley. There, in an area of spring-fed meadows abutted by red rock cliffs, he built the Big House, a dream home for his wives and children.

In the valley that surrounded his home, he laid out farm plots and built barns, corrals, a dairy, and a blacksmith shop. He became the region's leading citizen and its largest stock owner and farmer. The Big House became the focus of community life. Church services and school instruction took place in the Maxwells' spacious living room, and when the time arrived for square dances, the man of the house would lead the musicians on his violin.

Maxwell and his wives seem to have had great respect and affection for their Indian neighbors. Maxwell learned to speak the local Indian dialects, and the trust he won made his home a gathering place for trade, talk, and the resolution of disputes. His wives formed strong ties with native women and showed them their ways of sewing and cooking. As an outgrowth of these friendships, two Indian children became part of the Maxwell family.

The decision William Maxwell made in 1877 to leave Springvalley was surely a choice his three wives regretted. They and their children would never again enjoy anything resembling the comforts and advantages they had known in their Nevada valley. A family photograph taken six years later in front of their adobe home in Pleasanton, New Mexico, reveals both the hardships of pioneering and the loss of basic comforts and amenities sustained by the Maxwell family.

At that time Maxwell was an old man by the standards of the day, and he was not responding to a call from the leaders. He marched to a different drummer. His gaze was still on the remaining unsettled areas in the Southwest, and before he died, eighteen years later, his yearnings would lead him and his fami-

William B. Maxwell (far left), Lucretia (his first wife)
seated next to him, and other members of his family, ca. 1883

lies to establish additional Mormon villages in Arizona and New Mexico and, finally, in the states of Chihuahua and Sonora in northern Mexico.

Driving his livestock ahead, Maxwell first relocated in Panguitch, Utah, and then in Orderville, an experimental Mormon communal village in Utah where all property was pooled. He served as the foreman of Orderville's cattle ranches. The next move of his families involved a two-month midwinter trek to the Little Colorado River valley in northern Arizona, where he became an early settler in Springerville and Alpine. With its lush meadows, Alpine was a veritable stockman's paradise, but three years later Maxwell was moving on to what he apparently perceived as a greener valley in Pleasanton, New Mexico.

Maxwell's next move, ostensibly to escape possible prosecution for polygamy, took him in 1884 to Mexico, beyond the reach of U.S. marshals. Here he "threw up" a home and settled down for a few years in Colonia Diaz, a new Mormon village in Chihuahua. The last move came in 1891, when the Maxwells traveled with a party of Mormons over the Continental Divide to Sonora in search of a place to establish another new settlement.

The final day of this trek was Maxwell's seventieth birthday, and it was fitting that his friends let him drive the first wagon down a mountain to reach a site on the Bavispe River, which would be his final frontier home.

William Bailey Maxwell was a long walker and a long rider. On foot, on horseback, and from seats on slow-moving wagons, he saw huge slices of the West in its more or less pristine prime. Fur trappers, seeking monetary gain, harvested beavers in western rivers and transported their pelts to market in St. Louis. Maxwell, a settler's settler, left a different legacy: he took part in the founding of communities.

Jacob V. Hamblin (1819–1886) and Louisa Bonelli Hamblin (1843–1931)

Jacob Hamblin had many things in common with William Bailey Maxwell. Both were sons of the Midwest who, in their youth, had the experience of transforming forested wildernesses into productive farms. Both had a restless streak, and both thrived on the challenges of frontier living. Both viewed their Indian neighbors as brothers under the skin and tried to improve their lot. And both were sent out of Salt Lake City by Brigham Young to help establish colonies in an outback of his Great Basin Kingdom.

There were significant differences as well. Hamblin was not an ordinary Mormon colonist: the singular mission Young assigned him was to serve as an Indian peacemaker, and he labored in this vineyard for twenty-four years. And unlike Bill Maxwell, Jacob Hamblin was not a conventional Saint. He was a mystic who saw the hand of the Lord in his everyday life, and he let his conduct be driven by dreams, whisperings, and magical presentiments.

A tall, rawboned man with a catlike gait, Hamblin was born in Salem, Ohio, in 1819. At age seventeen he moved with his father to Wisconsin to help him clear land; then he worked in a lead mine and homesteaded. He converted to Mormonism in 1842 and moved to Nauvoo, then to Iowa, and in the summer of 1850 to Salt Lake City in a company of Saints led by Aaron Johnson.

When the Johnson company arrived in Salt Lake City that September, Brigham Young directed them to continue forty miles west and start a village, which would be known as Tooele, Utah. Here began Hamblin's lifelong interest in American Indians and their cultures. Shoshone Indians conducted sporadic raids on the new settlement, and Jacob Hamblin participated in a campaign to subdue them. However, since Mormon scripture taught that American Indians were "remnants of the House of Israel," Hamblin privately concluded it was wrong to kill them. Acting on his own initiative, he undertook a peace mission in which he "went alone into their country [and] remained with them for several days, hunting deer and duck."

The mystical insights he believed he had gained during this experience, Hamblin recounted later, "forcibly impressed me that it was not my calling to shed blood [of any Indians] but to be a messenger of peace to them. It was also manifest to me that if I would not thirst for their blood, I should never fall by their hands."

In April 1854, Brigham Young put flesh on his nascent Indian peace policy by sending Hamblin and twenty-two other missionaries to work among the frontier tribes in the south. Young was so impressed by Hamblin's work that he subsequently put him in charge of Indian peacemaking throughout southern Utah and northern Arizona.

Hamblin put his convictions about Indians into practice forthwith. Often operating alone, he visited the lodges and campfires of the Piedes and Paiutes to learn their languages and customs. When disputes developed, he "made it a specialty to go among them, regardless of their number or anger."

More than half of Young's missionaries returned to their homes after a season in the south, but Hamblin believed he had found his life's work, and in 1865 he "removed" his family to a far edge of this frontier on the Santa Clara River. Here, he and his missionary companions set out to create homes and a gathering place for native peoples in the region. They first built a small fort and then persuaded the local Indians to help build a dam and create rude canals so that corn, cotton, and other crops could be grown in adjacent bottomlands.

In August 1857, Young appointed Jacob Hamblin president of the Indian Mission and instructed him to implement his "conciliatory policy" with local Indians and "seek by works of righteousness to obtain their love and confidence." Hamblin was a quiet man who never became a prominent leader of his church, but his adventures as a peacemaker made him an icon for many Mormons.

Hamblin's horizons were altered by his new responsibilities. He took a second wife, seventeen-year-old Priscilla Leavitt, sister of a close friend; escorted California-bound emigrant trains through the deserts of southern Nevada; and soon widened the reach of his mission by following the valley of the Virgin River southward to the Colorado River.

One year later, the scope of Hamblin's mission was enlarged again when Brigham Young told him to cross the Colorado River and try to convert Hopi Indians to the Mormon faith. Hamblin's Indian friends guided him to the only place where, in low runoff, horses could ford the Colorado before it plunged into the cataracts of the Grand Canyon. This location, later celebrated as the "Crossing of the Fathers," had first been used by Europeans in 1776 when an exploring party led by Francisco Silvestre Vélez de Escalante, a Franciscan priest, cut rock steps in a steep sandstone slope so their horses could descend to the river and carry them back to Santa Fe.

Like the friars who preceded them, Hamblin and the missionaries who later worked with him found it difficult to interest the Hopi priests in the religious doctrines they espoused. After many visits, the Mormons finally persuaded three Hopis to cross the big river to visit their communities, but no baptisms followed. Neither Catholics nor Mormons seemed to grasp that the belief system of the Hopi clans was rooted in traditions that to them were stronger than the tenets of Christianity.

When an influx of Mormon immigrants transformed the region around Santa Clara into a bustling farm community, Hamblin decided, in 1869, to move east to an unsettled area called Kanab. Brigham Young, bent on creating a self-sufficient economy for his people, had sent large groups of Saints south to Santa Clara and St. George to produce cotton, tobacco, wine, and molasses in a region that would soon be called Utah's Dixie.

Hamblin's arbitrary decision to uproot his families from the homes and gardens they had built in Santa Clara underscores the harsh male-centeredness of Mormon theology of the time. In making this decision, Hamblin ignored the wishes of his two wives and the hardships that beginning a new settlement on the frontier would inflict on them and their nine young children. But he was not in the habit of listening to the hopes and desires of his "helpmates." Like most zealous Mormon men, he believed that if he put "the Lord's work" first, the Lord would take care of his families' needs.

The Hamblins moved to their new home in Kanab, a cabin in

Jacob Hamblin (center right) and John Wesley Powell (to his left) meeting with a band of Paiutes, by John K. Hillers, 1873 (Courtesy National Anthropological Archives, Smithsonian Institution)

Inset: Jacob Hamblin (Courtesy LDS Church Archives)

a stockade; their neighbors were a band of Paiute Indians, who became Jacob Hamblin's friends and worked with him as scouts and developers of the farmlands. For a year, Priscilla and Hamblin's fourth wife, Louisa Bonelli, lived with him far from other Mormons on this raw frontier. Brigham Young arrived the following September with a caravan of Saints, however, bent on establishing a Mormon outpost in the area.

Young was accompanied by Major John Wesley Powell, the famous scientist-explorer, who would form a lasting friendship with Jacob Hamblin. The previous year Powell had become a national hero when he led a daredevil expedition down the unexplored wild canyons of the Colorado River, and Congress had honored Powell by authorizing him to conduct a geologic survey in the vast region he had traversed.

Major Powell hired Hamblin as his guide, and they traveled together for several weeks. Mapmaking was the major's primary interest, but he also wanted to learn the fate of three boatmen who had left his starving expedition and climbed out of the Grand Canyon and into the Indian country southwest of Kanab.

Hamblin soon located the Shivwit natives who, it turned out, had killed the missing boatmen. In the course of a peace talk, he persuaded the Indians to describe the event that led to the deaths. Major Powell would later draw this word portrait of his new friend:

> This man Hamblin speaks their language well, and has a great influence over all the Indians in the regions round about. His talk is so low that they must listen attentively to hear, and they sit around him in deathlike silence. When he finishes a measured sentence, the chief repeats it, and they all give a solemn grunt.

To pave the way for subsequent scientific surveys on the Colorado Plateau, Powell was anxious to cross the river and establish ties with the Hopis and Navajos. Hamblin eagerly accepted Powell's offer to serve as guide and interpreter on this trip as well. The biggest threats to peace on Hamblin's frontier watch were raids by Navajo horse thieves on Mormon settlements. With help from Major Powell, the trip might give him an opportunity to discuss this problem with Navajo tribal leaders.

The results of a two-day conference at Fort Defiance exceeded Hamblin's expectations and would be a crowning achievement of his career. After a meeting of 6,000 Navajos was called to order by a U.S. Army officer, Powell introduced Hamblin and urged the Indians to heed the message of his friend, "the Mormon Captain." Hamblin began by presenting the war-or-peace alternatives facing the Mormons and Navajos; then he described his own dedication to "preserve peace between white men and Indians" and urged the Navajos to end their raids and come and visit and trade with his people.

Barboncita, the principal chief of the Navajos, gave a positive response the following day. Powell rose and hailed the success of the peace talks. Hamblin followed with assurances that he would welcome all Navajos who came to Kanab to trade blankets for horses. He concluded with a promise: "I guarantee safety on the other side of the river."

Hamblin's safety guarantee held firm until the fall of 1873, when three Navajos who had passed through Kanab on a trading mission were killed by a non-Mormon rancher. When he learned that angry Navajos blamed Mormons and were planning retaliatory raids on Kanab and other Mormon towns, Hamblin knew what he had to do: visit the dead men's enraged relatives and try to reason with them.

Hamblin crossed the river with two companions and found his way to a lodge where a Navajo war council was preparing to meet. His life hung in the balance during the dramatic twelve-hour trial that followed. The bloody shirt of the young Navajo who had survived the Utah massacre was waved in his face. Clan members who wanted revenge at first demanded a life for a life but later offered to compromise if Hamblin would deliver 350 horses to the aggrieved families.

One of Hamblin's companions, J. E. Smith, described his response: "Hamblin behaved with admirable coolness.... He reminded the Indians of his long acquaintance with their tribe ... and challenged them to prove that he had ever deceived them." When taunted with the question "Aren't you afraid?" Hamblin replied: "Why should we be afraid of our friends? Are not the Navajos our friends and we theirs? Else why did we place ourselves in your power?"

Hamblin's appeal changed the mood of the meeting, and he was allowed to go in peace after he promised he would return a month later to take his longtime friend the Navajo leader Hastele, along with other Navajo leaders, "into our country" to learn the truth about the death of the traders. The peaceful resolution of this dispute (without any input from Indian agents or government troops) marked the end of hostile confrontations between the Mormons and their Navajo neighbors.

It was honest, face-to-face talks that alleviated tensions and produced peace, and Hamblin later attributed the outcome to his "correct insight into Indian character." To him, the Indians in the region were brothers, not savages, and he believed disputes could be resolved when efforts were made to understand the natives' way of thinking and their reaction to events. His approach to peacemaking was simple: "I reason with an Indian as an Indian."

The opposite approach—sending a posse to kill or punish Indians accused of misdeeds—often produced injustices, he knew. He had witnessed such a tragedy during his Santa Clara days when an angry party of Mormons went on a punitive foray without him and executed two blameless Paiutes who were his friends.

When Brigham Young died, in the summer of 1877, Jacob Hamblin's health was failing and the goals of his Indian mission had been achieved. He promised Priscilla and Louisa, his two living wives, that he would spend more time performing the duties of a father and making their lives more comfortable.

But his promises were not kept. Hamblin's yearnings to see new country, not calls from church officials, led him to uproot his wives and children three more times in the last eight years of his life.

These post-Kanab years were not a happy or prosperous time for Hamblin and his family. He first moved south with Priscilla into Arizona's White Mountains. Later, he built a ramshackle home for Louisa in Pleasanton, New Mexico, and then lived with her in Chihuahua for a year or two. By the time malaria claimed his life in Pleasanton in the summer of 1886, his meager resources had dwindled and his wives had to rely on their children for support.

Jacob Hamblin played a prominent role in western settlement, and his zeal for this was so all-consuming that he put an inordinate burden on his wives. Stories told by my great-grandmother, Louisa Bonelli Hamblin, his youngest wife, provide some insight into the stresses and strains the institution of polygamy imposed on Mormon women.

Pearson H. Corbett, Hamblin's biographer, informs us that after the death of his first wife, Lucinda Taylor, Hamblin set out to "marry as soon as possible" in order to ease his second wife's (Rachel Judd) "heavy load" of bringing up all nine of his children. Corbett concedes that it "looked like a business proposition" when Hamblin, with undue haste, approached George Bonelli to ask for the hand of his attractive daughter. Bonelli at first objected but subsequently relented.

There are intimations that real love never blossomed, but Louisa seems to have adopted an Old Testament "whither-thou-goest" approach to her marriage. Her children remembered her as a dutiful wife and mother who kept the faith and rarely complained about her lot. But Louisa lived for almost a half-century after her husband's death, and in her old age she commented to one of her granddaughters, "I was not happy unless I was miserable, for I knew nothing except hardships." And at a Sunday dinner after a Mormon preacher had recounted her husband's deeds as a peacemaker and informed the congregation she was Jacob Hamblin's wife, she wryly observed, "He should have said Jacob Hamblin's squaw."

Levi Stewart (1812–1878) and Margery Wilkerson Stewart (1832–1870)

Until his death, Brigham Young's "calls" shaped the lives of thousands of Mormon families. As we have seen, his decisions determined that William Maxwell and Jacob Hamblin would be itinerant pioneers and serve as outriders of the Mormon advance in the southland.

Levi Stewart's early experiences were similar to those of Maxwell and Hamblin, but his Utah life followed a different path. A tall, handsome man whose dark hair and blue eyes made him stand out in a crowd, Stewart was blessed with business acumen that enabled him to become a pillar of Salt Lake City's commercial establishment.

Soon after arriving there in 1848, Stewart began to make his mark as an entrepreneur. He established a general merchandise store in a choice location, and the business flourished. He went on to build two large homes in the city, send his children to private schools, and provide his family with season tickets to the soon-to-be-famous Salt Lake Theatre. He also gained the respect of Brigham Young, who asked him to accompany him on inspection trips to new colonies and came to rely on his counsel in developing Utah's unique economic system. Among other accomplishments, Stewart is credited (by historian Leonard J. Arrington in *Great Basin Kingdom*) with helping to resolve Utah's 1858 currency crisis.

Stewart's comfortable citified life came to an end in the spring of 1870 when Young directed him to lead a company of twenty families to develop a village at Kanab. Although Stewart was now an old man and had forgotten many of the frontier skills he had acquired in the 1840s, he had lost none of his religious faith.

He promptly sold his families' homes and disposed of the businesses he owned. In April that year, his party left Salt Lake City on a 300-mile journey that was interrupted only by a stopover in Pipe Spring to plant crops they could harvest later. By mid-June, his missionaries were building temporary shelters and digging a system of ditches that would enable them to divert water from Kanab Creek to irrigate gardens and orchards they planned to plant the following year. Already, Stewart was on his way to building a thriving community.

Stewart's swift rise as a leader in the commercial life of the Mormon community, first in Salt Lake City and then in Kanab, raises fascinating questions. What, one wonders, were the qualities that enabled this frontier farmer to transform himself into a leader of Utah's emerging business community? It is clear that he was a man (in the Mormon parlance) "whose word was his bond," and the quality of his business decisions apparently inspired confidence in his customers and associates.

There are also indications that Stewart prospered because Brigham Young realized early on that he was a venturesome leader interested in importing technologies that would enhance

Utah's economic future. Young's respect for Stewart's business acumen was apparent as early as 1856, when the church organized the Brigham Young Express and Carrying Company, the largest economic venture undertaken in the first decade of Utah's history. Stewart, at Young's request, became an officer of this effort to link Missouri and Utah with a speedy commercial transportation system, and the investments Stewart made helped ensure the success of the venture. Later, when the church was having problems establishing a paper industry, Stewart was asked to import the latest machinery from St. Louis and set up a modern paper mill on his Cottonwood Canyon property.

Levi Stewart continued in this brand of pioneering when he settled in Kanab. On that far frontier, he imported and installed the first steam-powered sawmill in nearby Arizona and encouraged his teenage daughter Ella (my grandmother) to master Morse code and serve as the territory's first telegraph operator.

In 1871, when Brigham Young came to inspect the town, he praised the settlers' efforts and appointed Levi Stewart as their bishop. Three months later, however, a calamity occurred that cast long shadows over the lives of the Stewart family. A dispatch Stewart telegraphed to a Salt Lake City newspaper described what happened:

> One of the most heart rending scenes took place on the morning of the 14th about 4:30 A.M., resulting in the death of my wife, Margery, and her sons Charles, Heber, and Edward; also my sons Levi H. and Urban Stewart who perished in the flames. Although there was a guard on at the time, he failed to know anything about it, until the cry of fire by myself, at which time two rooms were in a light of flame. Seven boys were sleeping in the back room, two of whom escaped thru the flames, there being no other opening to the room. My wife, Margery, rushed through the flames to waken her children, and perished before

Margery W. Stewart, 1854

there was a chance of rescue; . . . all perished by the explosion of the coal oil which was stored in the room with them.

In the sorrow-filled weeks after this "fearful dispensation of Providence," Stewart's friends urged him to give up his mission and resume life in Salt Lake City. However, he decided to stay. He built a fine home for his wife Artimacy, Margery's younger sister, and spent the remaining seven years of his life as a frontier father and community builder.

John Doyle Lee (1812–1877) and Emma Batchelor Lee (1836–1897)

The controversial John Doyle Lee, my great-grandfather, was a ground-floor Mormon who was a member of Brigham Young's inner circle during the flight from Nauvoo and the exodus to Utah. In a secret temple ritual Young had adopted Lee as one of his celestial sons, and he relied on Lee to carry out critical assignments in this turbulent period of Mormon history.

Born in 1812, John D. Lee spent the first sixteen years of his life in the vicinity of Kaskasia, Illinois. His maternal grandfather, John Doyle, a soldier in the army of George Rogers Clark, had taken part in the 1778 raid that captured the British fort at Kaskasia, and he returned a few years later to help settle this outpost on the Mississippi River.

Orphaned at age three, Lee was raised by his Doyle relatives. He had only three years of formal education, but as a teenager he acquired experience as a farmer, became a skillful horseman while serving as a mail carrier in southern Missouri, learned the art of wagonmaking while in the employ of an uncle, and worked as a clerk and bartender in the mining town of Galena, Illinois.

Lee was first exposed to Mormonism in 1838 when Levi Stewart, a neighbor in Vandalia, Illinois, loaned him a copy of *The Book of Mormon*. He and his wife, Agatha Ann Woolsey, soon joined the church, sold their home, and moved to western Missouri, where they erected a cabin near the homes of the Stewart brothers. A few weeks later, conflicts erupted that led Governor Lillburn W. Boggs of Missouri to declare that Mormons should be "treated as enemies and must be exterminated or driven from the state."

Lee had gone to Missouri as an inquiring convert, but by the time he moved his family back to Illinois a year later, his experiences and the persecutions he had witnessed had intensified his belief in Mormon doctrines. He had laid his life on the line for the church, he had been exalted on hearing Joseph Smith's charismatic sermons, and he was now armed with convictions that, for the rest of his days, would make him a willing servant of those presiding over the Saints' earthly affairs.

By 1843, Lee had established a home in Nauvoo and gone on five proselytizing missions to Tennessee and nearby states. As an evangelist, he had preached to more than 1,000 people and baptized more than 100 converts. He had also avidly embraced

Joseph Smith's new doctrine of plural marriage. By May 1845 he had taken five additional wives, including my great-grandmother, Lavinia Young, a woman he converted in Tennessee.

By the time Lee evacuated his families from Nauvoo in the spring of 1845, he had established himself in Brigham Young's eyes as a stalwart lieutenant. Two decisions Young made in Iowa while the Mormons were planning their westward trek reveal the trust he placed in John D. Lee. In August, he asked Lee to overtake the Mormon Battalion in Santa Fe and pick up its payroll. Lee accomplished this perilous mission and made the round-trip in three months. Later, when wintertime food supplies were dwindling, at Young's request Lee took a wagon train to St. Joseph, Missouri, and used payroll savings to purchase bulk supplies of food the Saints would need to survive.

After Lee made the trek to the Great Basin in 1848 and put down roots in the headquarters of the new Zion, he had good reason to believe that Brigham Young might give him a leadership position in the church hierarchy. He had won his spurs as a doer, he was Young's adopted son, and during his first year in the valley, when the Council of Fifty exercised wide powers as a virtual municipal government, he had served as that group's secretary. Lee was surely disappointed when, two years later, Young ordered him to move 300 miles south into wild country to help establish an iron industry. But he did not complain. Obedience to authority was a cardinal tenet of Mormon doctrine, and Lee was a zealot who never questioned decisions made by the man he esteemed as God's prophet on Earth.

Lee loaded his wagons and headed south with two of his wives and a small company of settlers. In a matter of months, he and his companions had selected a townsite—later named Parowan by Brigham Young—built a fort, constructed makeshift cabins for their families, and shoveled ditches to carry water to newly planted fields. Soon thereafter, Lee sold his property in Salt Lake City and moved his other wives and children to new homes in Parowan. He went on to found the village of Harmony 100 miles southwest of Parowan near the Old Spanish Trail, traversed by California-bound emigrants. Young sent twenty young men to serve as Indian missionaries there and directed them to work with Lee to erect a new outpost, Fort Harmony, nearby.

When Lee moved his families to Fort Harmony in the winter of 1855, it appeared they might finally be establishing permanent abodes. Young made Lee probate judge in the newly created Iron County and appointed him the region's "Indian farmer," with authority to distribute tools and seeds to natives of the area and teach them the rudiments of irrigation farming. Lee also became a major in the Iron County militia, a unit organized and commanded by the leaders of the Mormon Church who presided in Parowan and Cedar City.

The Mountain Meadows Massacre

One of the most abhorrent episodes in the annals of western history is the massacre carried out in the Mountain Meadows, a valley in southern Utah, in early September 1857. Blunders by panicky leaders created the whirlwind that made this senseless slaughter possible. President James Buchanan, one of the most inept chief executives in the nation's history, triggered a tragic sequence of events in July of that year by announcing that he was sending an 800-man army from St. Louis to Utah to quell a "rebellion" in that territory.

Brigham Young, his mind on the persecutions and drivings of the 1840s, overreacted by assuming that this force was being sent to uproot and exterminate the Mormons. In Utah's first decade, he was the head of a theocracy and functioned in a dual role as governor of the territory and president of the church, and he also served as commander of the Nauvoo Legion, the territory's militia. Young fostered hysteria by using Armageddon rhetoric and announcing resist-unto-death war plans.

Young activated Mormon militias, ordered his soldiers to build redoubts on the approaches to Salt Lake City, and told families to prepare to evacuate their homes and move into tent towns in the mountains. If Buchanan's troops entered the Salt Lake valley, he warned, they would find the city, its houses, and the fields in ashes.

A caravan of California-bound emigrants from Arkansas led by Alexander Fancher and Captain John T. Baker arrived in Salt Lake in early August and moved southward toward the Old Spanish Trail as the Mormons' fears and suspicions were being whipped to a fever pitch. The thirteen families who made up the caravan were looking forward to a quiet, uneventful journey and posed no threat to the peace and security of Mormon communities. Children under the age of sixteen outnumbered the men, and eighteen infants, ranging in age from six days to six months, outnumbered the women in the wagons.

The Fancher-Baker party was preparing to leave Utah in early September when their camping place in the Mountain Meadows was turned into a killing field. It was not long before the massacre was shrouded in rumors that it had been the work of angry Indians.

With a heavy heart, I have pored over almost everything that has been written about the massacre. I have also had long conversations with people in Utah and Arkansas who have sought to understand the events of that fateful week. My analysis of the available evidence has forced me to conclude that Indians were not involved in the massacre and that it was the work of a well-organized Mormon militia.

What actually transpired can be surmised if the myth of Indian participation is rejected. Acting under orders, some militiamen disguised as Indians and led by Major John D. Lee ambushed the wagon train and killed or wounded several emigrants. The Arkansas men circled their wagons and fought back. Three days later, the commanding officer of the Iron County militia, apparently fearing big trouble if the Fancher-Baker party were allowed to move on to California, mustered his fifty-man troop and issued an order to "put away" all the emigrants except the infants.

When the militiamen were assembled behind a hill near the Mountain Meadows, a treacherous scheme was approved by the field commander, a colonel. Lee was one of the emissaries chosen to carry a white flag and an offer to "rescue" the emigrants from any further "Indian" onslaught. Under the plan presented, the men would surrender their guns and the company would then be escorted to safety in Cedar City. The infants would travel ahead in a wagon; the women and children would walk in a separate group; and following at a distance, the men, each guarded by an armed militiaman, would march in a long column. Desperate to save the lives of their women and children, the leaders of the wagon train accepted these terms.

Once the wagon filled with infants was out of sight, the commander on horseback called a halt and gave a signal, whereupon each militiaman shot his male hostage at close range. Then, in a melee of terror that lasted only minutes, the soldiers advanced and slaughtered the women and children.

What took place in the aftermath is well documented. The bodies of the slain were hastily dumped in shallow graves. The infants were parceled out to Mormon families. And the booty (wagons, horses, oxen, 600 head of cattle, and personal valuables) was apparently put in the custody of local church leaders.

As whisperings and questions multiplied, leaders of the militia spread word that Indians had massacred the emigrants and that the soldiers sent to the Meadows had arrived too late to save

John D. Lee, 1857
(Used by permission, Utah
State Historical Society, all
rights reserved)

the adults. Two weeks after the massacre, John D. Lee, at the urging of the militia's officers, traveled to Salt Lake City and presented what became the standard version of this canard to Brigham Young and his counselor Wilford Woodruff.

Lee's oral report is well documented. According to him, the Fancher-Baker party had done "evil things" that enraged the Indians. He reported that it took the natives five days to kill the men and then they had slit the throats of the women and children. The Indians had spared eight or ten infants and then "sold" them to the Mormons. He himself had personally taken some men to the Meadows and interred the bodies of the emigrants.

Where his church superiors were concerned, Lee's cover story was immaculate: he said nothing about the involvement of the Iron County militia or the decisions made by its commanders. But the Indian story did not ring true, and federal lawmen suspected the massacre was the work of Mormon soldiers. As a result, federal judges and prosecutors appointed by the president of the United States began to investigate, and outraged Arkansas relatives demanded that the surviving infants be identified and returned to their relatives.

Alarmed that rumors about the massacre could besmirch the reputation of his church, Brigham Young had the apostle who supervised church matters in southern Utah investigate and render a private report on the incident. This document provided whitewash that allayed his fears. It supported the Indian massacre story and at the same time appeared to condone the massacre on the specious ground that members of the Arkansas party might have been connected with the Missouri and Illinois drivings. Moreover, after three days of soft questions, the apostle cleared all leaders of the militia except John D. Lee of any involvement in the murders at the Meadows.

When federal officers went south the next spring to take custody of the infants and gather facts, they conducted a midnight interview with one conscience-stricken militiaman. He confirmed their suspicions. They also heard various Indian massacre stories from others in the area that did not hang together. A few months later, the nation got its first grisly glimpse of the atrocity when an army cavalry troop en route to Utah from California passed through the Mountain Meadows and found the valley strewn with human bones and scraps of clothing. When federal officers went to arrest the militia leaders they suspected were behind the slaughter, however, their mission was thwarted: forewarned, the men had repaired to hideouts in the mountains.

National interest in the massacre mystery waned when the Civil War began. As a result, life in this far-off frontier flowed back into normal channels in the 1860s. John D. Lee prospered. He built homes for his wives, helped found a new colony in the Virgin River valley, and converted a family kitchen in New Harmony into a tavern for travelers en route to southern California.

Lee also remained in Brigham Young's good graces during this period. Young performed the marriage rite when John took Emma Batchelor as his seventeenth wife, and Young invited him to join his entourage for pastoral visits to the southern settlements.

First-generation Mormons took pride in describing themselves as "a peculiar people," and isolation from outside influences was vital to maintenance of their distinctive way of life. The idyllic separateness of the Great Basin Kingdom ended in 1869, however, when stations of the first transcontinental railroad were located in Ogden and Salt Lake City. Now journalists and noted travel writers such as Horace Greeley and Richard Burton could study the settlers' culture. Their reports about aspects of plural marriage caused a sensation and stirred anti-Mormon sentiment in the nation that triggered a twenty-year campaign to stamp out polygamy.

Brigham Young's teachings, his multiple wives, and the strict control he exerted over his flock put him in the spotlight, and in short order Mormon-bashers were accusing him of ordering the Mountain Meadows massacre and shielding its perpetrators. Realizing that some response was necessary, Young had John D. Lee excommunicated. This edict turned Lee into an outcast and put the burden of responsibility for the massacre on his shoulders. Lee, now on a slippery slope as a scapegoat and fugitive from justice, frantically sought a hearing, but Young's resident apostle rebuffed him with a curt note that said: "Our advice is to trust no one. Make yourself scarce and keep out of the way."

Although he surely realized he had been singled out as a sacrificial lamb, Lee nevertheless believed his precious membership in the church would ultimately be restored. Thus, when Young ordered him to establish a ferry to transport immigrants and their wagons across the Colorado River in order to found new Mormon colonies in northern Arizona, he viewed it as a chance for redemption. The assignment made him singularly scarce, for the ferry site was located in one of the most remote, lonely tributary canyons in the region.

Without the devotion and fortitude of two of his wives—Rachel and Emma—Lee would not have been able to carry out this formidable undertaking, which, under the direction of Emma, continued a few years after his death. Today, remnants of the crude shelters he and his wives and children erected at Lee's Ferry and at Jacob's Pools bear witness to the hardships that marked the fulfillment of this important church mission.

Even though he had been cast out, John D. Lee retained affection for Brigham Young, and he considered it a benediction when Young sent him a message praising his efforts "in advancement of our settlements." He left his labors on the river and was granted a private audience with his old friend. According to his journal, Young's parting words were, "John, you must be careful and stand by your integrity." It was to be their last meeting.

Finally captured in November 1874, Lee faced two murder trials in federal court. The first resulted in a hung jury when all eight Mormons voted for acquittal. This outcome inflamed anti-Mormon sentiment, and Brigham Young and his advisors apparently decided that if Lee were sacrificed, the controversy over the Mountain Meadows atrocity might subside.

When prominent Mormons appeared as the main witnesses at the second trial a year later, it was clear that a deal had been made. On the surface, Jacob Hamblin presented the most damaging testimony against Lee, but his testimony was rank hearsay: he had been far away in northern Utah when the massacre occurred. This time, an all-Mormon jury took less than an hour to decide that Lee was guilty.

Lee rejected the counsel of friends that he jump bail and seek refuge in Mexico. He also rejected the prosecutor's offer of a plea bargain that would allow him to go free if he gave evidence that implicated Brigham Young in the massacre. A year later, John D. Lee was taken back to the Mountain Meadows and executed by a firing squad.

A Personal Postscript

Brigham Young died a few months later, and as far as the law and the Mormon Church were concerned, Lee's execution closed the book. However, it opened a book of unending anguish for his wives and children. As did many other family members, John D. Lee's son David Lee (my grandfather) fled southern Utah. He put down roots in the high country of western New Mexico, married one of Jacob Hamblin's daughters, and became a successful cattle-man. At their farewell, his father said, "Don't waste your time defending me," and throughout his life David ignored arrows of criticism and rarely discussed the Mountain Meadows tragedy, even with his children. The church's hard-edged version of the massacre was taught in Sunday school classes, and Lee's progeny learned to either walk out or bite their tongues during these "history lessons."

I remember, as a youngster, seeing the pain on my mother's face as she awkwardly explained the meaning of "scapegoat" and described what had happened at the Meadows. I remember, too, the chill I felt in the 1940s when I read a blunt summation written by Joseph Fielding Smith, a Mormon apostle who doubled as the church's official historian: "[The massacre] was the crime of an individual, the crime of a fanatic of the worst stamp."

My mother was overjoyed in 1950 when Juanita Brooks, a Mormon historian who had lived all her life in southern Utah, published the first exhaustive, dispassionate study of the massacre. Brooks documented how this atrocity had evolved out of "a complex chain of circumstances that involved many people." It was a group crime, she concluded, executed under military orders, and she traced the tortuous process by which Lee was ultimately singled out as the leader who carried out the massacre.

In 1989, two magnanimous men approached me and I was drawn into the vortex of a tragedy that had seethed with hostility and suspicion for 132 years. Verne Lee (a relative) and Ronald Loving (a Fancher descendant) had formed a friendship and had been working with the families to bring about a reconciliation in southern Utah, where a memorial service for the victims was to be held. This was a highly sensitive undertaking, and Verne and Ron soon realized that two conditions had to be met if their efforts were to bear fruit: in a nonaccusatory environment, a spirit of forgiveness had to prevail, and leaders of the Mormon Church had to be present and participate.

I went with Verne and Ron to present this concept to Gordon B. Hinckley, president of the Mormon Church. He agreed not only to participate but also to lend his influence to a plan to erect a marble monument overlooking the Meadows.

In September 1990, this culminated in a private meeting of more than 200 descendants of the families, who came from far and near to attend. The ceremony took place at a large auditorium in Cedar City. Prayers were offered and hymns sung, and Rex E. Lee (then president of Brigham Young University, former solicitor general of the United States, and my cousin) spoke for the Lees. Judge Roger Logan and J. K. Fancher represented the Arkansas families, and Hinckley expressed his church's sorrow and remorse for what he called an "inexplicable tragedy."

For me this was a poignant, searing experience. I wept at the ceremony, and I still weep every time I read the names of the women and children who were wantonly slaughtered. I shudder every time I contemplate the terror they felt in the last moments

THE MOUNTAIN MEADOWS (1990)
for Louise Lee Udall (1893–1974)

There was a massacre in these hills.
Four generations have come and gone,
but the deed that haunted the children
that haunted the lives of the militiamen
hovers over the silent land.

Now descendants of the slain
and sons and daughters of the slayers
come, arm in arm, to end the tragic story,
to share a burial rite, perform a
ceremony of atonement.

But how to cleanse the stained earth?
To erase old griefs and grievances?
To quench long-dying embers of anger?
To forgive unforgivable acts?
The balm they bring is love,
the only ointment God offers
To heal wounds too deep for healing.

—Stewart Lee Udall

of their lives. This is what forced me to study everything I could
find that threw light on the massacre. Among my conclusions
were these:

• The families in the Arkansas caravan were blameless.

• The massacre, from beginning to end, was the work of the Iron

County militia—and the incredibly stupid, inhumane decision to exterminate the travelers was made by the commanders of that military unit.

• There is no credible evidence that Brigham Young was involved in the massacre decision.

• Except perhaps as scavengers, Indians played no part in the massacre, and it was cruel and immoral for the Mormons to saddle them with blame for it.

Emma Lee and the Endurance of Settlement Women

John Lee's story is one of the most dramatic and better documented of the settler generations, and just as with the exaggerated attention given to Old West gunslingers, in the focus on men like Lee it is easy to overlook the extraordinary contributions to settlement of pioneering women, such as John Lee's seventeenth wife, Emma.

A native of Sussex County, England, Emma Batchelor was twenty in May 1856 when she joined the Mormon Church and sailed from Liverpool with a company of Utah-bound converts. Emma was a strong, adventuresome person, and it is likely she would not have flinched had she known her life in the New World would take her to remote regions of the western frontier and confront her with uncommon tragedies and triumphs.

After a train ride from Boston to Omaha, Emma and her companions became part of an unprepared "handcart company" that a leader sent up the Mormon Trail so late in the summer that they almost perished in the Rocky Mountains when trapped by unseasonable snowstorms.

A woman with an abundance of stamina and strength, Emma

Emma B. Lee, ca. 1890

probably saved the lives of one family by keeping them moving, pulling and pushing the flimsy two-wheeled wooden carts that contained their food and clothing up the trail. Luckily, a rescue expedition from Salt Lake City arrived in time to prevent large-scale loss of life and help the suffering immigrants complete their 1,000-mile trek to their promised land.

The course of much of Emma Batchelor's subsequent life was determined a year later when she married John D. Lee and joined his families in the hills above the Mountain Meadows, on the Old Spanish Trail to California.

When, in 1872, knowing that federal lawmen were intent on capturing those responsible for the Mountain Meadows massacre, Brigham Young assigned John D. Lee the task of establishing a ferry across the Colorado River, it was Emma who stayed with Lee as companion and partner. She named their new home in this secluded location Lonely Dell, and during his long absences she operated the boat at what became known as Lee's Ferry.

When Lee was finally arrested and jailed in central Utah, Emma continued to run the ferry and sent some of the proceeds to help pay for his lawyers. One traveler who saw Emma in action praised her in his journal for the skill and "great courage" she exhibited as she handled a skiff and rescued cattle that had fallen overboard into the icy water of this turbulent river.

For two years after Lee's execution, Emma continued to operate the ferry. In 1880, she married Frank French, a prospector, and moved with her children to Winslow, Arizona, a ramshackle new town constructed by the company that built the Santa Fe Railroad. There, Emma learned the rudiments of frontier medicine and soon carved out a new career for herself by providing medical care for her neighbors. Tragedy continued to dog her family life, however. Her daughter Victoria committed suicide at age fourteen, and her second son, Ike, was murdered by a cowboy who coveted his wife.

Putting her talents as a midwife to good use, Emma soon became a pillar of the Winslow community. She not only maintained a "hospital" in her home for expectant mothers but also applied her general medical skills and carved out a role as her community's only doctor. She persevered in this role until 1897, when she died at age sixty-one. The editor of the local newspaper wrote of her life: "She was filled to overflowing with the milk of human kindness. No matter how inclement the weather, or what the hour of the day or night, she was always ready to respond to the call of the afflicted, whether rich or poor."

On the rugged margins of the frontier, few men met challenges—or made contributions to settlement—comparable to those of Emma Batchelor and the many women like her.

These stories of Mormon settlers may in some aspects be atypical, but they illustrate in a general way the hardships most settlers encountered and the courageous, tenacious responses of so many first-generation settlers of the Old West.

II Settlement in the Old West: Correcting the Record

3 Explorers and Fur Trappers

"On every page [of *Across the Wide Missouri*] we hear the sound history makes when it is written by a spoiled novelist in love with what he writes about."

—Wallace Stegner

*D*id the crude, colorful frontiersmen who made a living killing beavers in the Rocky Mountains play a paramount role in the settlement of the West? Should mostly illiterate trappers be considered witting "agents of empire" working to expand the reach of a political entity whose ideas and intentions they did not comprehend? Is it reasonable to present men who demonstrated little interest in creating communities as farsighted individuals who played crucial roles in the settlement of the American West?

The late Bernard De Voto provided affirmative answers to such questions in three best-selling and highly influential books he wrote in the 1940s and early 1950s. De Voto's frontier trilogy— *The Year of Decision* (1943), *Across the Wide Missouri* (1947), and *The Course of Empire* (1952)—won prizes and established him with startling speed as a leading authority on vital aspects of western history.

De Voto's ascent was especially surprising because, though a well-known literary critic and editor who also made part of his living as a novelist (under a pseudonym), he had never composed a work of history. His bravura debut as a historian can be attributed to his masterful writing and to his ability to transform raw materials of history into exciting folk dramas. De Voto believed that "history was surcharged with romanticism," a conviction that unfortunately led him to ignore ordinary settlers in his accounts and build his stories around scenes and characters he deemed more colorful.

The elder Arthur Schlesinger, then a pioneer in the new field of social history, thought that De Voto's entertaining tomes were pseudo-histories. However, his historian son, Arthur Jr., welcomed De Voto's narratives as "buoyantly novelistic" and praised the writer's "open appropriation of the devices of fiction." Where conventional historians assembled facts and used them to bolster conclusions, De Voto began by developing sweeping generalizations and then marshaled facts to support his synthesis. De Voto's readers would have been surprised to learn that he was essentially an armchair historian. He once admitted that he had had no interest in western history until he left the West and, in fact, had never seen most of the landscapes he described in such vivid prose. More particularly, the son of a Mormon mother and a Catholic father, De Voto came to manhood with contempt for both religions and their role in the West, and he seldom looked back after he shook Utah's dust off his feet and headed east to Harvard University.

The technique De Voto used to transform frontier trapper Jim Bridger into a Bunyanesque leader of western expansion is typical of his method. It is on display in *Across the Wide Missouri*, for example, in his description of Brigham Young's 1847 encounter with Bridger at the latter's trading post on the Green River in

Wyoming. Bridger doubted that the Mormons could grow enough food to sustain themselves in the Great Basin and advised Young to stay on the Oregon Trail and find a suitable location for settlements to the west. Here is De Voto's fictionalized description of this meeting:

> Drums should have rolled and trumpets sounded, or the supernatural stage management of this millennial creed should have provided signs from on high, for the Mormons had now met the master of these regions, their final authority. Apostle Smith had brought in Old Gabe, Jim Bridger. . . . His was the continental mind and the pilgrims of eternity were children come a little way into the kingdom of Old Gabe. As a monarch he instructed them. . . . Bridger became the oracle of revelation and when the time came, Brigham would be able to speak the Lord's will and say, "This is the place."

The conversation between Bridger and Young occupies a hallowed niche in Mormon folklore. The story Young's companions remembered and recorded in their journals was simple and direct. Brother Brigham was searching for a lean environment that would not be coveted by other immigrants—a sanctuary where his flock could labor unmolested to turn deserts into gardens. The Great Basin fit his vision of the Lord's promised valley, so Young brushed aside Bridger's advice and instructed his wagoneers to turn southward and follow the wagon tracks made the previous year by the Donner party into that vast expanse of untrammeled country.

It was pure theater for Bernard De Voto to present Bridger as a rustic monarch armed with the insights of a geopolitician. In his exuberance, De Voto overlooked a landmark truth of western history. The individual who had distance in his eyes in the summer of 1847 was Brigham Young, not Old Gabe. Young had a vision that was regional in scope, and a clear concept of what he hoped his people could accomplish. Bridger soon faded away— only to be rescued and canonized later by writers such as De Voto. But by the time Young died, in 1877, his vision had been translated into a Mormon "commonwealth" of settlements that embraced a land area extending 1,000 miles from north to south and 800 miles from east to west.

De Voto developed three overarching themes to place his heroes at center stage. The first involved a contention that at some point in late 1845 or 1846 there was a "sudden acceleration of social energies" that quickened emigration and galvanized interest in expanding the country's boundary to the Pacific Ocean. The second was his conclusion that these social energies broadened the gaze of most Americans and produced a "continental mind." His third theme was that Jim Bridger and other fur trappers were fore-runners who led the way to the conquest of Oregon and California and thus deserve recognition as farsighted "agents of empire."

The evidence does not support such a "great leap" hypothesis. It is not credible, for example, to transform fur trappers, who spent their days in the wilderness killing animals, into political seers. Nor is it plausible to imbue these wandering backwoods-men with visionary political ideas or to pretend they were point men of an imperialistic campaign when their contacts with the political entity known as the United States of America were, at best, tangential.

Besides, if one excludes Mormons (who trekked west to escape the confines of the United States), definitive statistics about travel across the plains do not support De Voto's theory that the pace of westward migration abruptly accelerated in 1845 and 1846 or that most Americans went west motivated by the idea that they were part of a national campaign to "change the destiny of the nation."

In truth, most of the early pioneers who went west in wagons were animated by personal motives linked to religious convictions. But, as the following passage reveals, De Voto's mind was closed to this possibility; instead, he declared that a semi-mystical impulse built of the doctrine of Manifest Destiny was tugging at the minds of the first-wave immigrants:

> The immigration was underway. Its great days were just around the turn of spring—and an April restlessness, a stirring in the blood, a wind from beyond the oak's openings, spoke of the prairies, the great desert, the Western Sea. The common man fled westward. A thirsty land swallowed him insatiably. There is no comprehending the frenzy of the American folk-migration. God's gadfly had stung us mad.

It was characteristic of Bernard De Voto that when he developed a thesis, the opinions he espoused to buttress it were flamboyant and final. In one of his tributes to the trappers, De Voto, an outspoken agnostic, surprised his friends with the predestinarian statement that "Providence was using [them] for no mean purpose." He also declared that they were "instruments of the nation's will," and he outlined the trapper legacy in this extravagant sentence: "The mountain fur trade had made [the land] known, opened it up, blazed the trails, located the water and the grass, named the rivers, triangulated the peaks, learned how to traverse the Great American Desert."

Then, leaving no base untouched, he fashioned this apotheosis for his three favorites, Bridger, frontiersman Thomas Fitzpatrick, and Kit Carson. These supermen, he opined, deserved recognition as "conquerors, makers and bequeathers of the West."

These encomiums presented a misleading picture of the pageant of western settlement. De Voto's omissions were far more important than what he recorded. The real story of settlement was a story of work, not conquest. Some native groups had created stable village societies in various regions of the West before the first Europeans arrived; the other main makers of the American West were the wagon families who carved out roads and built homes in hundreds of valleys, with very little assistance from Bernard De Voto's bequeathers.

De Voto's Indians

There is no evidence in his narratives that De Voto made any effort to understand the cultures and lifeways of American Indians. As a result, his work is permeated with racism and steeped in stereotypes peddled by Wild West writers, all of which distorts the authentic history of the American West. In preparing the script for his trilogy, De Voto viewed the West's Indians as savages blocking the path of his Manifest Destiny parade.

Historian Gary Topping noted an "immense irony" in the fact that *Across the Wide Missouri,* the second volume of De Voto's trilogy, was at its inception a historical sketch designed as a commentary on the work of three artists—Alfred Jacob Miller, Charles Bodmer, and George Catlin—who chronicled the life and culture of the Plains Indians. Yet, as Topping notes, none of these artists had a racist outlook, and their paintings present a "more accurate picture of the Indians than De Voto ever did!"

De Voto was a master of the sweeping generalization, and the opinions he expressed about native peoples were invariably dogmatic and degrading. With a magisterial air, he pontificated that the Sioux were "a neolithic people." The Plains Indians were "the most savage on the continent." The Apaches, he opined, were a "vigorous and cruel race." The Comanches were "professional marauders and murderers who were practicing sadists." And although De Voto conceded that the Pawnees were intelligent, he put them down as "expert thieves, liars and extortionists."

In short, De Voto viewed the West's natives as a subhuman species who were obstacles to progress. He recounted, for example, that when Joseph Walker, one of his heroic trappers, encountered a band of destitute, unarmed Root Digger Indians on his way to California, he "wiped them out . . . as he would have stepped on piss-ants." And he declared that the natives in Oregon's Willamette River valley who were about to receive the ministrations of Methodist missionaries were Indians "whom forty years of lay effort had already made into white men about as much as was possible, which is to say they were degenerate, debauched, diseased, despairing and about to die."

De Voto's harsh, monolithic view of native cultures caused him to overlook the vital contributions western Indians made to the fur trade and the vital aid they provided to companies of wagon settlers in the first perilous years of migration. Had he evaluated the experience of the Hudson's Bay Company with native trappers or studied the mutually beneficial relationships Charles and William Bent developed with Plains tribes at their trading post in southern Colorado, he would have discovered that it was the Indians, not the trappers, who located most of the original trails in the West.

A remarkable book written in the 1970s by a young historian, John D. Unruh Jr., presents findings and conclusions that puncture balloons inflated by De Voto and other mythmakers. This comprehensive work, *The Plains Across: The Overland Emigrants and the Trans-Mississippi West, 1840–60*, offered many new insights for students of western history. After a decade spent studying thousands of letters, diaries, memoirs, journals, and newspaper and periodical accounts, Unruh mustered evidence that gives a fresh, compelling picture of interactions between Indians and settlers during the overland era of wagon migration.

Unruh's findings reveal, for example, that the natives and

whites "had an infinite variety of encounters" and were not implacable enemies. He explodes the Wild West myth that there was "incessant warfare between brave overlanders and treacherous Indians." And his documentation reveals that many groups of pioneers relied on Indians to guide their wagon trains, to help them harvest food, and to provide other life-sustaining services.

Indians actually provided more valuable aid and assistance to westering migrants than did the trappers, Unruh concluded. His research also demonstrated that on the trails to Oregon and California from 1840 to 1860, more immigrants killed Indians than vice versa. Here is his fascinating account of what he found:

> The extent of Indian attacks on overland caravans has been greatly exaggerated. In fact, there is considerable evidence that the fatal trail confrontations which did occur were usually prompted by emigrant insults and disdain for Indian rights, as well as by indiscriminate and injudicious chastisement meted out by the U.S. Army. Notwithstanding the fact that nearly 400 emigrants were killed by Indians in the first twenty years of overland travel, Indian tribes provided overlanders with information, foodstuffs, clothing, equipment, horses, canoeing and swimming skills, traveling materials and other assistance.

The evidence John Unruh amassed offered an antidote to a century of overblown, anti-Indian rhetoric. He presented a cogent argument for a fundamental change in attitude toward aboriginal peoples, and he ripped a hole in Bernard De Voto's tent of heroes. His research revealed that some of the trappers ordained as "makers of the West" actually stationed themselves along the Oregon Trail and fleeced wagon families who were headed west. A young Bostonian, Francis Parkman, witnessed the ruthless plundering of immigrants in the summer of 1846 when he stopped at Fort Laramie. "In one bargain, concluded in my presence," Parkman noted, "I calculated the profits that accrued to the fort, and calculated that at the lowest estimate they exceeded eighteen-hundred per cent."

Manifest Destiny and the Early Pioneers

De Voto held a harsh view of all religions, and he did not mince words in characterizing what he saw as the aims and endeavors of the people of faith who trudged across the plains to bring their teachings to the natives. To his mind, they were by and large zealots who had detached themselves from the real world:

> No one will ever tell in full the heroism or the stupidity of the foreign missions, the holiness-saturated devotion of the missionaries or their invincible foolishness. There were only two agencies for the extension of civilization on a large scale, armies and missions, and in the light of history the primitives who drew the armies were much better off. The missionary was a man glad to submerge self in a holy cause, but except in a minority so small it does not count, his dedication locked him away so completely from reality that at this distance he seems crazed, if not crazy. The heathen were not people to him: they were souls.

In the process of glorifying his Manifest Destiny version of western history, De Voto began espousing a religion of his own, and perhaps he thought he had to discredit the efforts of religious folk in order to protect the validity of his doctrine. At times, the rhetoric he used to sell his gospel of national expansion seemed to hail the presence of a secular Holy Ghost. In one fervid passage, for example, he declared that when "history writes tragedy in the grand manner, the lives of human beings [are] in pawn to the foreordained."

De Voto embellished his notion of predestination at another point when commenting on the decision of the Reverend Jason

Lee, one of Oregon's early pioneers, to continue to Oregon and not turn north to Montana. De Voto announced that he acted as "an instrument of national will" and, donning the robes of a secular seer, proclaimed that "Lee gave the orders but Manifest Destiny cast the vote."

De Voto's chauvinistic concept was such an integral part of his histories that it was apparently unthinkable for him to concede that all western missionaries might have had a will of their own and a plan to acquire land and build homes before they began serious proselytizing. He condemned them out of hand because they did not fit into the pigeonhole he had prepared for them. With this purple prose he transformed them into unwitting agents of empire:

> The missionaries were vortices of a force thrown out in advance by the force to the eastward that was making west. They thought they came to bring Christ, but in thinking so they were deceived. They were agents of a historical energy and what they brought was the United States. The Indians had no chance. If it looked like religion it was nevertheless Manifest Destiny.

In his effort to make the missionaries, willy-nilly, foot soldiers of Manifest Destiny, De Voto spouted faulty history. His assertion that the natives were accorded better treatment by the U.S. Army than by churchmen, for example, is simply outlandish, as anyone would know who has studied the nation's nineteenth-century Indian policies. Not only were religious leaders in the forefront of the fight against President Andrew Jackson's Indian removal apartheid plan in the 1830s, it was men of the cloth who led the campaign for the abolition of slavery, who provided the moral thrust that forced President Ulysses S. Grant to initiate an ill-fated Indian "peace policy," who in many regions provided hospitals and schools for natives decades before a laggard federal government began to supply such services.

One wonders whether De Voto was so attached to his Manifest Destiny gospel that he failed to realize that the U.S. Army was a minor presence in the West until after the Civil War. Was he not aware that during and after that conflict (in an era when General Philip Sheridan, who was in command of western "pacification," announced that the only good Indian was a dead Indian) the history of the West was blackened by inexcusable military massacres of Indians?

Had De Voto been interested in making a dispassionate analysis of nineteenth-century missionary endeavors, he would have studied the approach New England Methodists followed in Hawaii, pondered what the Moravians did to help the Cherokees in Georgia, and examined the unique ecumenical relationships worked out between Franciscan friars and the Pueblo Indians in the Southwest. Had he carried out such research, De Voto might have come to recognize that it was the contributions of early immigrants motivated by religious convictions that initially made it possible to expand the reach of democracy in the American West.

De Voto and the Mormons

The Mormons presented Bernard De Voto with a particularly pesky problem of interpretation. He had been exposed to a heavy dose of Mormon history while growing up in Ogden, Utah. He knew that the Mormons were, in effect, thrown out of the United States and went west not as conquerors but as refugees searching for a homeland. He knew that their motivation had no connection whatsoever with Manifest Destiny agitation in the East. And he must have realized that when it came to colonization, Jim Bridger and the other fur trappers contributed little to settlement in the Great Basin.

Since the accomplishments of the Mormon pioneers constituted at least a glaring exception to his primary themes, De Voto
could not ignore this distinctive chapter of western history. In
trying to find a terse way to deal with their exceptional hegira, he
decided to use a backhanded approach. Although he had a low
opinion of Brigham Young's character, he knew historians would
look askance if he failed to acknowledge Young's achievements as
a colonizer and temporal leader. De Voto resolved his dilemma
with one crisp sentence. Brigham Young, he opined, was "a great
leader, a great diplomat, a great administrator, and at need a
great liar and great scoundrel."

In his cavalier treatment of the Mormon saga, De Voto
revealed his general disinterest in the broader grassroots story of
western settlement. Yet he could have found compelling drama in
the wide-ranging saga of Mormon pioneering, for in the first
decade after they arrived in the Salt Lake valley, Young and his
devoted followers established ninety-six far-flung communities,
stretching from Lemhi in northern Idaho to San Bernardino in
California.

Since there was no way such a story could be folded into his
Manifest Destiny matrix, De Voto elected to interweave dramatic
scenes with pompous descriptions of the lives of a few Big Men.
It was thus inevitable that he would submerge the work of thou-
sands of Mormon settlers by simply proclaiming that Brigham
Young "gave the Great Basin to the United States."

The trappers and explorers were important, but by magnifying their achievements De Voto wittingly obscured the bedrock
contributions of the wagon settlers who came before and after
these men he glorified as pathfinders.

4 The Religion Factor in Western Settlement

"Upon my arrival in the United States, the religious
aspect of the country was the first thing that struck
my attention."

—Alexis de Tocqueville

*A*n elemental but often unacknowledged truth
about the settlement of the American West is that the basic
ground breaking was, in large measure, the work of religious
groups. Much of the confusion surrounding western frontiering
has been an outgrowth of the simplistic concept of Manifest
Destiny and the unending flow of clichés it has spawned. Over
time, this glittering doctrine created a haze that obscured the piv-
otal role religious groups played in determining the outcome of
western settlement.

For more than three centuries after the Age of Exploration got
under way in 1492, venturesome Europeans established colonies
on far-flung continents and islands, where they mined precious
metals and harvested sugar, spices, tobacco, and other products for
home markets. For much of that time, however, a vast area that
would come to be known as the American West lay beyond the
reach of all but the most intrepid of these colonizers. This land-

locked region was larger than western Europe, and it was kept nearly inviolate by its remoteness and intimidating terrain.

The land west of the Mississippi River still appeared on maps as "unknown country" when, for example, President Thomas Jefferson sent Meriwether Lewis and William Clark on their storied overland expedition to the Pacific Ocean in 1804. Aside from an awareness that this westerly land was Indian country and that Spain maintained European settlements in far-off Texas, New Mexico, and California, there was sparse information in the newly formed United States about the geographic features of this region.

Spain's mariners had first mapped the wild coasts of Oregon and California in 1542, and two years earlier Francisco Vásquez de Coronado had scoured the mountains and plains from the Grand Canyon to eastern Kansas in search of fabled cities of gold. But the Spaniards had not shared details about these early discoveries. The early Spanish settlements that did take hold about fifty years later were religiously inspired, and the same can certainly be said about the bulk of subsequent early migrations west, though these were inspired more often by Protestantism and Mormonism than by Catholicism.

The Catholic Settlements

The Catholic colonizing that began in the Rio Grande valley of New Mexico occurred almost exactly two centuries before the Lewis and Clark expedition first focused the minds of Americans on the scope and scale of the landmass their nation had purchased from France. In evaluating the achievements of Spain's missionaries in the seventeenth and eighteenth centuries, it is important to remember two crucial facts: First, this was an epoch of militant Christianity, and the monarchs who ruled Spain during these centuries were devout Catholics who viewed conquest and conversion as an intertwined undertaking. Second, inhospitable environments in parts of the Southwest made missionizing a particularly daunting task.

New Mexico, for example, was situated 1,000 miles from the capital of New Spain. For more than two centuries, there was so little traffic between Santa Fe and Mexico City that the Franciscan friars and settlers lived in a kind of time warp, with only sporadic contact with their mother civilization. Yet the dedication of these sons of Saint Francis was so fervid that in their first thirty years, they interacted with Pueblo people by establishing a string of twenty-five missions near their villages, in an arc that stretched from Pecos, New Mexico, to the Hopi villages in Arizona.

ARIZONA

Of all the regions in the United States colonized by Spanish Catholic pioneers, the Sonoran Desert in Arizona presented the most formidable obstacles. Both Indian and Spanish settlement in this land of little rain was confined to valleys where spring-fed streams provided a permanent source of water. This area was also the homeland of aggressive Pima and Apache Indians, who raided the villages of sedentary natives and harassed the tiny garrisons New Spain maintained on the Sonoran frontier.

The challenges of this spare environment were met by an exceptional leader, Father Eusebio Kino. A vibrant Italian who had joined the Jesuit order, Kino requested in the final years of the seventeenth century that he be sent on a "distant and dangerous mission." Kino got his wish: he was to spend the rest of his life in a wedge of the Sonoran Desert that stretches from Arispe, in Sonora, to Yuma and to the San Pedro River in eastern Arizona.

Eusebio Kino and his Jesuit companions began by converting natives and helping them build churches and plant gardens in small valleys in northern Sonora. Undeterred by the harsh cli-

Father Eusebio Kino, as
memorialized in National
Statuary Hall, Washington, D.C.
(Courtesy Architect of the
Capitol)

mate of his diocese, Kino next eyed the desert mountains on the horizon and dared to believe that, armed only with love, he could mount a horse and discover new lands and peoples and at the same time serve his Lord by extending the boundaries of Christendom. His vision—and his ability to command the affection and loyalty of the native peoples he encountered—made him a preeminent pathfinder and mission builder in the West.

In the final two decades of his life, Kino made forty pack trips and traveled 8,000 miles to map new areas and bring messages of peace to the natives. In the company of Indian neophytes who served as his vaqueros, the tireless "padre on horseback" visited all the valleys and Indian villages in the cactus country of Sonora and southern Arizona.

Father Kino is rightly esteemed as Arizona's founding father. A peacemaker, he won the loyalty of the native peoples by deeds rather than words. An advocate of improved gardening methods and animal husbandry, he took steps to provide Indian communities in the Santa Cruz and San Pedro River valleys with herds of cows, sheep, and goats, along with seedlings for orchards. His actions gave him such a wide reach that Herbert Bolton, the historian who pioneered the study of Spanish borderland history, informs us that when Kino's superiors sent an order assigning him to go on a mission to Baja California, "the authorities of Sonora protested on the ground that through his influence over the natives, he was a better means of protection to the province than a whole company of soldiers."

"Eusebio Kino was the most picturesque missionary pioneer of all North America—explorer, astronomer, cartographer, mission builder, ranchman, cattle king and defender of the frontier," suggested Bolton. And he left an expansionist legacy. Having memorized his region's shorelines, streams, and landmarks, he prepared the first maps of this huge area and marked sites for future missions. Before he died, in 1711, he had developed plans for missionizing that would determine the pattern of Indian and European settlement in Arizona. And his pioneering set in motion developments that led to the founding of Tucson in 1776.

Before Spanish rule ended in 1821, energetic friars and devoted native craftsmen put a capstone on Kino's work by building majestic chapels in the desert at Tumacácori and San Xavier. These churches stand today in timeless beauty as expressions of the unquenchable faith that animated the missionaries of the Kino epoch.

TEXAS

Franciscans who fled south from Santa Fe after the Pueblo Rebellion of 1680 created the first Texas missions along the Rio Grande below El Paso. These successes turned Franciscan eyes to other areas of Texas, and by 1714 a large mission had been established at San Antonio. By the time this effort peaked in the 1750s, nearly fifty missions and several small presidios had been created in a vast arc that extended from San Saba on the western plains of Texas to Laredo to Goliad to Nacogdoches in eastern Texas.

There were failures, and some nascent settlements had to be abandoned, but missions that thrived encouraged more Spanish families to immigrate and create villages in well-watered valleys. Texas natives in some areas readily acquired agrarian skills. An observer who visited the San Antonio mission in 1772 reported that the natives had cattle, sheep, and goats "in abundance" and had become so adept at farming that "without the aid of Spaniards they harvest, from irrigated fields, maize, beans and cotton in plenty, and Castilian corn for sugar."

In the last decades of the eighteenth century, Spanish pioneering in Texas began to lag, mainly because Spain, now Europe's economic sick man, did not have the resources to support vigorous colonizing and provide a respectable military presence in Texas. The hardy mission settlements that did survive into the nineteenth century were, however, sufficient to sustain the sovereignty claims of Spain and Mexico to Texas. Where settlement was concerned, it was the Franciscans' pioneering that encouraged English-speaking people from the United States to immigrate to Texas in the 1820s, when it was still part of the Republic of Mexico.

CALIFORNIA

Mission building by Franciscan friars along the California coast commenced in 1769, with advantages that would have amazed Father Kino and his inland brothers. With cargoes delivered by ships, the missionaries sent to California had from the first the tools, animals, and supplies they needed to complete their projects on schedule.

These padres had other advantages as well. A beneficent climate guaranteed that farms and orchards would bear rich harvests and that grasslands would support large numbers of grazing animals. Moreover, the pacifist traditions that permeated the lives of most coastal natives ensured that missionary endeavors would seldom be disrupted by attacks.

The colonizing of the Spanish province of California that began in 1769 was the work of Father Junípero Serra, a university-trained native of Majorca who founded a mission at San Diego. Serra began building a second mission at Monterey the following year, and by the end of 1771 he and the sixteen Franciscan priests who shared his burdens had broken ground for missions in northern California at San Jose, in central California near the San Antonio River, and in southern California at San Gabriel.

About the same time, Spanish officials in Mexico City were pondering the strategic importance of San Francisco Bay, and Viceroy Antonio Bucareli y Ursúa decided to strengthen Spain's presence in the north by establishing a colony in that location. In the winter of 1776, Captain Juan Bautista de Anza, a Sonoran military officer, led a company that included thirty families with 118 children and 1,000 head of livestock on a 1,600-mile overland trek from Culiacán across the Mojave Desert and northward to the San Francisco Bay Area. These venturesome colonists founded a community in Santa Clara. Until a revolution in Mexico ended Spanish rule in 1821, the colonists' sons and daughters worked with the friars to create several additional communities in northern California's lush valleys.

Father Serra was a firm, dynamic leader. He and his Franciscan friars did not come to California to help expand Spain's empire; their singular aim, according to their lights, was to expand the domain of their faith. The pattern of missionizing Father Serra and his brothers established effectively determined California's Indian policy, its settlement plans, and the lifestyle of its colonists. During California's mission period, the church—in the form of Serra's Franciscan order—virtually functioned as the state in this vast territory.

Before his death in 1784, Serra founded nine missions extending from Santa Clara to San Diego. He also established authoritarian rules that governed the conduct of mission activities and regulated the lives of thousands of California natives who were forced or persuaded to live in villages that surrounded his missions.

By the time Mexican patriots expelled their Spanish rulers a few decades later, a Franciscan cadre of fewer than sixty priests had created an extraordinary ecclesiastical domain in California. The order's tightly run missions now numbered twenty-one, with 31,000 natives living in compounds clustered around them. There were several inland missions, six in the San Francisco Bay Area and one in the Sonoma Valley, in the northern part of the Bay Area. The missionaries also had effective control over the territory's arable land and maintained a herd of 750,000 livestock.

Throughout the twentieth century, there was a slow-burning controversy over Father Serra's Indian policies. Historian Herbert Bolton once hailed the accomplishments of the Franciscans by describing their missions as "great industrial schools" where "women were taught to cook, sew, spin and weave; the men to fell the forest, build, run the forge, tan leather, make ditches, tend cattle and shear sheep."

However, a young writer, Richard Henry Dana, described the natives as serfs after observing their living conditions in the 1840s. Latter-day critics, pursuing Dana's theme, have viewed the missions as a plantation system in which native peoples were treated like children, were never allowed to leave, and thus could not use their newly acquired skills to build independent villages where both Christian and traditional values could be cherished. Other critics, noting that hides, tallow, shoes, saddles, and other goods were exported to garner funds to expand the missions, have argued that all too often ideals of Christian brotherhood were sacrificed to meet economic imperatives.

Whatever view ultimately prevails, it is undeniable that pre–gold rush California was transformed by the pioneering work of the Franciscans. The animals they brought into the region, the concepts of farming and ranching they introduced, and the crafts they taught using European tools and techniques added elements of European civilization to what had been a wilderness environment.

The influence of these advances was never acknowledged by the gold-crazed hordes who crowded into California during the 1850s. Overnight, these newcomers fashioned a myth that "gold made California." This jingoistic legend became a gaudy curtain that obscured the importance of the incipient civilization the friars had created. Moreover, it would have been impossible to feed and sustain the throngs of gold seekers if productive farms and ranches had not already existed—and if wagon transportation and rudimentary port facilities had not been available when the famous stampede began.

The Franciscans were forced to abandon their missions and withdraw from California in 1821 as a result of the anti-clerical policy of the Mexican Revolution. Even though their mission system collapsed when they departed and the churches, abandoned to the elements, fell into decay, the roads, farms, and ranches they had built provided a vital infrastructure for California's incoming populations.

The Pacific Northwest

The Catholic Church's final missionary endeavor on the western frontier began in 1841 when a resourceful Jesuit priest, Father Pierre-Jean De Smet, responded to the entreaties of a Flathead Indian delegation and traveled with them from St. Louis to their homeland in Montana's Bitterroot River valley. Affectionately called "the Blackrobe" by the natives, De Smet was an idealist who ventured into the Far West believing that he could establish independent Indian colonies patterned after the renowned "reduction" the Jesuits had developed two centuries earlier in Paraguay. The Paraguayan experiment had been based on a utopian premise that if a secluded valley could be located, tribal cultures could remain intact there and Christian teachings could be blended with the native spiritual concepts.

On a trip down the Columbia River, Father De Smet found that Jesuits from Quebec were already building chapels and serving the religious needs of Canadian Métis (individuals of mixed American Indian and European descent) who had trapped beavers for the Hudson's Bay Company in the Oregon Country. After consultations with his brothers, he decided to recommend that his concept of utopia in one valley be enlarged to encompass the whole Columbia River area. De Smet sent glowing reports to his superiors in St. Louis and Rome about the "great harvest" he envisioned if his plan were adopted.

Father De Smet was a visionary with a level of energy that astonished his peers, and he readily garnered support for his ambitious plan. On returning to St. Louis, he was authorized in 1843 to embark on a fund-raising trip to Europe. His efforts were a huge success, and he gained the approbation of the leader of his order. After recruiting priests and purchasing supplies, he hired a ship in Antwerp to transport his company around Cape Horn to a port on the Columbia River.

De Smet's dream was clothed in moral majesty, but it did not take into account the rapid changes swirling across the West in the 1840s as the United States Congress voted to annex Texas and start a war with Mexico. His superiors soon saw shortcomings in De Smet's plan and, in 1846, abruptly canceled it. Viewing the West from St. Louis, where sentiment for "removal" of natives was overwhelming, the Jesuits in charge were aware that secluded valleys were disappearing and that the rising tide of migration into and across the Great Plains would, perforce, produce conflicts by shrinking the Indians' homelands and undermining their cultures.

De Smet's work as a western colonizer was thus cut short when the Jesuit hierarchy withdrew its support. The candle he had lit in the Pacific Northwest flickered out, and he spent his remaining decades in St. Louis, where he wrote books, helped found a university, and attended peace parleys with tribes in the valleys of the Missouri River.

At the behest of federal officials, De Smet played a role in negotiating dubious treaties with the Lakotas and other tribes. But he surely witnessed the unfolding of the Indian tragedy on the Great Plains with fatalistic misgivings and realized that the promises embodied in hasty agreements would not be kept unless the national government changed its approach and took positive steps to help natives preserve their cultures and hold on to their homelands.

If Father De Smet's legacy as a missionary is ambiguous, it is because, unlike Helen Hunt Jackson in California, he did not speak out against the racial animosity and the injustices he witnessed. Instead, he became part of the St. Louis establishment and hobnobbed with its politicians and military men. The career the father pursued in his later years emboldened historian Elliott West to characterize him as a "secular agent of an expanding nation."

Protestant Colonizing

Activities by Protestant churches that led to settlements in frontier areas of the West began in Hawaii in 1820. The overall Protestant effort was an outgrowth of what Sydney Ahlstrom, the preeminent chronicler of religious life in America, described as "the immense evangelical energy that was loosed on New England and America" in the early 1800s. Historians have called this revival the Second Great Awakening.

The evangelical episode known as the First Great Awakening, identified with the thinking and sermons of the Reverend Jonathan Edwards, had reached its culmination in the 1740s. In the nineteenth century, the aspirations fostered by the Second Great Awakening had far greater influence on the nation's culture and values. The zeal it generated encouraged citizens to elevate the quality of life in their communities and enlarge the meaning of the liberties they had won.

In the first decades of the nineteenth century, the fervor generated by the Second Great Awakening led to a proliferation of temperance societies and many other voluntary associations formed to improve American life. The most successful of these entities involved "education societies" formed to promote Christian dogmas. These groups encouraged the establishment of Sunday schools and disseminated tracts and children's books decades before public school systems were created. Few American historians have acknowledged the vital contributions religious folk made to America's development in the nineteenth century. An observant Alexis de Tocqueville, writing in 1835, assessed the powerful influence churches at the time were exerting on social and political affairs in this country:

> Religion in America takes no direct part in the government of society, but it must be regarded as the first of [that country's]

political institutions; for if it does not impart a taste for freedom,
it facilitates the use of it.

Tocqueville was fascinated by the influence of evangelical
societies Protestants were organizing to increase their outreach.
In 1810, an interdenominational group formed the American
Board of Commissioners for Foreign Missions, which sent pros-
elytes as far away as China and Burma. A few years later, the
Methodists' American Home Missionary Society sent missionaries to Hawaii to work with the Polynesian people in the Sand-
wich Islands.

The Hawaiian experiment had prospered because the
Methodists respected the culture of their hosts and operated on
the assumption that the performance of baptismal rites marked
the beginning of a gradual process of religious instruction.
Hawaii subsequently became a model for American proselytizing
when the Methodists sent doctors, teachers, ministers, printers,
and farmers to help native-born Hawaiians improve their lot.
The establishment of schools, the creation of a Hawaiian alphabet, and the development of institutions of self-government followed in due course.

About the time Tocqueville completed his American travels
in 1832, Protestant missionary societies were considering propos-
als of enthusiasts who wanted to establish missions somewhere in
the Columbia River basin. Inspired by their experience in
Hawaii, in 1834 the Methodists led the way by sending the Reverend Jason Lee, his nephew Daniel, and four companions on an
overland trek to explore the outlook for missions in the area
vaguely described as the Oregon Country.

Lee was an ideal choice for this assignment, and he founded
the first American settlement in the Oregon region. A physical
giant, as an outdoorsman and pioneer builder he was fearless,

resourceful, and indefatigable. More important, he was a cogent, passionate spokesman for his causes. When he went east in later years to raise funds for his missionary work, he never returned to Oregon empty-handed.

Not to be outdone, the year after Lee went west, the interdenominational American Board of Commissioners for Foreign Missions sent out a two-man exploring party consisting of the Reverend Samuel Parker and Marcus Whitman, a young physician who aspired to be a medical missionary. Moving west in the company of trappers, these two eventually arrived at the Columbia River and were attracted by a promising site west of present-day Walla Walla, Washington, in the homeland of the Cayuse Indians.

Parker decided to winter over in the West. The impatient Whitman, now an experienced frontiersman, chose to return immediately to his home in upstate New York to muster more support for his wilderness mission. In August, with two young Nez Percé Indians as companions, he rode east to pursue his quest for funds and fellow missionaries.

Whitman's zeal generated action on several fronts. By the time spring arrived, he had secured the financial support he needed and had recruited Henry Spalding, an ordained minister, to meet him in St. Louis and join his small Oregon-bound caravan. He and Spalding each made a last-minute decision that improved the prospects for their pioneering in Oregon. Whitman persuaded Narcissa Prentiss to marry him and travel west with him. Narcissa was a devout, high-spirited woman, and events would make these two the best-known missionary couple in western history. Spalding married Eliza Hart, a frail woman who agreed to put her faith in God and share her husband's missionary adventures.

Armed with substantial contributions from the faithful,

Whitman outfitted his party in fine style. In addition to purchasing extra clothing, tools, saddles, a tent, and ample supplies of staple foods, he acquired fourteen horses, six mules, four milk cows, thirteen beef cattle, and a heavy farm wagon. The Whitman party straggled west in the company of a caravan of fur traders, arriving at the Walla Walla River in mid-September. Discussions and scouting trips led to the decision to establish two separate stations. Whitman's settlement was founded five miles west of today's city of Walla Walla. With the encouragement of friendly Nez Percé Indians, Spalding located his mission in Idaho, at Lapwai.

While Whitman was engaged in his own travels, Jason Lee was busy enlarging the Methodists' domain in the Willamette River valley. Lee had initially arranged for reinforcements to arrive by sea from Boston via Honolulu. This roundabout voyage took almost a year, but in May 1837 five women, three men (a carpenter, a blacksmith, and a doctor), four children, and a hefty cargo of supplies arrived at an Oregon landing.

Having won his spurs as a pioneer, the next year Jason Lee took five young Indian converts with him on an overland trek to publicize the accomplishments of his missions and to persuade his board of commissioners and the Methodist congregations to support a large expansion of the Willamette colony. Lee's stirring lectures and sermons about the potential for saving souls in Oregon's wilderness inspired Methodists to contribute the unprecedented sum of $40,000 for his ministry. The sailing ship he chartered attracted wide publicity when it embarked from New York in October 1839. Aboard, along with Lee and his new wife, were fifty-one women, children, and men, among whom were teachers, doctors, farmers, and six clergymen.

In large measure because of the pioneering of Protestant missionaries, by 1842 Oregon loomed as a land of promise in the minds of thousands of Americans. Stories in the religious press, a book by Samuel Parker, and tantalizing newspaper stories made this once-forbidding region appear as a West Coast Eden accessible to venturesome men and women.

Reports of the accomplishments of Lee, the Whitmans, the Spaldings, and the missionaries who were laboring with them in the Oregon vineyard excited the imagination of restless individuals. Oregon emigration societies were organized in the East on the basis of several perceptions:

- That families could load their belongings on wagons and travel in caravans all the way to the Oregon Country.
- That women and children could endure the rigors of an 1,500-mile wilderness hegira and cross the plains in safety.
- That missionaries would be available to help arriving immigrants find land and build homes.
- That it was feasible for settlers to take cows and other domestic animals with them to Oregon. Historian David Lavender underscored the significance of this development by observing: "[Those] who had made the monumental journey were not wild trappers but humble missionaries driving with them that most homely of domestic adjuncts, milk cows and calves. No trail over which a cow has once trudged can ever again seem wholly awesome."

The Protestant missionaries who blazed the Oregon Trail and converted it into the nation's first transcontinental roadway laid the foundation for larger companies of wagon families to move overland beginning in 1843. The significance of this churchly achievement is underscored when one realizes that before the Civil War the national government did very little to make the strenuous overland journeys of westering pioneers safer or less arduous.

The Protestants' civilizing efforts in the Oregon Country did not stop with the creation of churches, schools, and communities. The first colleges and universities in this region were founded by denominations decades before Oregon's first secular university opened its doors in 1876. Foremost among these fledgling institutions of higher learning were Willamette University (Methodist), founded in 1842; Pacific University (Congregational), in 1849; Linfield College (Baptist), in 1849; and Lewis & Clark College (Presbyterian), in 1867.

The Mormon Outreach

As noted earlier, the towering figure of Brigham Young—and the cohesive ecclesiastical matrix of Mormon life in the nineteenth century—affirms that the settlements in the expansive region the Mormons colonized merit a unique niche in the annals of American history. Of the Mormon ethos, Leonard J. Arrington, author of *Great Basin Kingdom,* a magisterial economic history of the Church of Jesus Christ of Latter-day Saints, noted: "It represents one of the few regional economies in modern history founded for a religious purpose, dominated by religious sentiments, and managed by religious leaders."

The story of the Mormons' trek to Utah has a sharp edge that punctures a gaping hole in the Manifest Destiny balloon kept aloft by the puffings of five generations of western writers. Having already been forcibly expelled from three states, when their prophet was assassinated in Illinois in the winter of 1846, the Mormons fled across the icebound Mississippi River into Iowa, where their leaders decided to leave the United States and find a secluded place beyond the Rocky Mountains in Mexico where they could live in peace.

What motivated the Mormons as they planned their exodus had no relation to the putative political destiny of the United

States of America. Mormons were Old Testament folk who believed they were taking part in a pageant of *divine* destiny. Words that became a mantra during their trek were those of Isaiah's prophecy:

> And it shall come to pass in the last days,
> That the mountain of the Lord's house
> Shall be established in the top of the mountains,
> And shall be exalted above the hills;
> And all nations shall flow unto it.

Within months after the Mormons were established in the Great Basin, Brigham Young had dispatched scouting parties to locate valleys that could sustain settlements. As creators of new communities, energetic Mormons excelled on several counts. The reach of the ninety-six settlements they initiated in their first decade in the Salt Lake valley is astounding.

By 1857, the outer boundaries of the Mormon theocratic kingdom stretched from San Bernardino, California, to the Carson River valley in western Nevada to Lemhi on the Salmon River in Idaho to Moab, Utah, near the Colorado border. The area of Mormon colonization embraced almost one-sixth of the landmass of what is now known as the lower forty-eight states.

In his *Religious History of the American People*, Sydney Ahlstrom cites Mormonism as "a witness to the possible social potency of prophetic religious ideas." With their wide-ranging settlements in diverse desert and mountain environments, Mormons demonstrated what could be achieved in the nineteenth century when an ardent Christian community strove to fulfill a destiny promise by its religious leaders.

The foundations for the settlement of the West were laid by religious groups. Yet this stirring chapter of the nation's history was obscured when, amid the clamor generated by the Mexican War, Americans came to believe it was military force that had opened the West for settlement. By the summer of 1848, when the generals—four of whom would subsequently be elected president of the United States—had dismounted their horses, legends about "the militaristic winning of the West" were already hovering over the nation's history, and "Manifest Destiny," the glib slogan begat by that war, was becoming a byword of American speech.

5 The Manifest Destiny Morass

"Manifest Destiny and imperialism were traps into which the nation was led in 1846 and 1899, and from which it extricated itself as well as it could afterward."
—Frederick Merk

A New York editor, John L. O'Sullivan, coined the expression "Manifest Destiny" during the spirited public debate that preceded the Mexican War, and thereafter this jingoistic catchphrase has skewed interpretations of western history. O'Sullivan was a propagandist with a penchant for extravagant ideas. The exuberance that characterized his writing is on display in the following statement, written at the end of 1845:

> [It is America's] manifest destiny to overspread and to possess the whole of the continent which Providence has given us for the development of the great experiment of liberty and federative self government entrusted to us.

O'Sullivan's credo added excitement to the ongoing debate over America's proper role on the continent when journalists and politicians made his conceit part of the national dialogue. Some even bragged that Canada, then a British Crown Colony, was destined to fall into the orbit of the American republic. Others predicted that the new nation of Mexico would shortly become part of the United States, either by conquest or by purchase. And a bevy of bellicose congressmen called the "western war hawks" fashioned a boundary war cry, "Fifty-four Forty or Fight" (referring to 54°40′ north latitude), based on the far-fetched assumption that the chanting of their slogan would somehow force the British Lion to cede to the United States its dominion over the Oregon Country and the area later known as British Columbia.

Because it had a messianic shimmer and brought giddy images of imperialism into the national dialogue for the first time, the "doctrine" of Manifest Destiny gained adherents during the Mexican War. Vapors from this political movement muddled perceptions of important western events and processes for years to come. History was ill served by effusions of the Destiny doctrinaires. They fostered confusion by suggesting that the settlement of the West did not commence until the late 1840s, when politicians made "great" decisions during President James K. Polk's administration. And in concentrating attention on land grabbed by marching armies, they belittled the importance of the settlements wagon pioneers had already established in the West.

The muscle-flexing by proponents of Manifest Destiny encouraged mythmaking. A legend that became embedded in history books held that the United States "won" title to the Oregon Country in the course of a "struggle for empire" with England. This was a canard. England was the world's military superpower in the 1840s. Her leaders were consolidating Great Britain's grip on the Indian subcontinent, and preparations were already under way to enlarge the nation's globe-girding empire by adding New Zealand and Hong Kong to it.

Having only a minuscule economic stake in this remote North American region, Great Britain had no reason to covet ownership of the Oregon wilderness. The conventional view that the Oregon-Canada boundary question involved a grand struggle for empire has always been an illusion. No hostilities were envisioned by either side. When the time came, a compliant President Polk meekly acquiesced to the terms of a treaty drafted in London by England's foreign secretary, George Hamilton-Gordon, fourth earl of Aberdeen.

Seen whole, the West was not "conquered" by feats of marching armies. American hegemony was established on the ground, not by decisions of far-off political leaders. In large measure, the West's future was shaped by courageous men and women who made treks into wilderness and created communities in virgin valleys. And the foundations for lasting settlements were laid by religious groups, not by soldiers. It is clear, too, that had there been no war with the feeble Republic of Mexico, in a few years New Mexico, California, and the Great Basin region would, like Texas, have come into the union of states as incoming settlers from the East came to dominate life in these areas.

To dispel the haze that hovers over the story of western settlement, it is important to understand the mood and the aims that guided the nation's attitude toward expansion before the doctrine of Manifest Destiny created confusion. An analysis of the ideas and policies that prevailed during the Age of Andrew Jackson provides especially valuable insights into these aims.

The Jacksonian Legacy

A Tennessee pioneer, Andrew Jackson was the first U.S. president from beyond the Appalachian Mountains. Jackson was a dynamic political leader, and his presidency marked a turning point for democracy in the nation. He presided over the extension of voting rights to at least some ordinary citizens (i.e., to white males) and the creation of modern political parties.

In his eight years in the White House (1829–1837), Jackson did not push for expansion of the country's boundaries. As president, he focused his energies instead on domestic issues and avoided disputes over slavery that would divide his political party. Jackson and his handpicked successor, Martin Van Buren, favored expansion through the gradual admission to statehood of territories created earlier by acts of the United States Congress.

The Age of Jackson was thus a relatively inward-looking period when Washington, D.C., lawmakers argued about tariffs and changes in the nation's financial policies. In the 1830s, Americans were excited by internal improvements such as the building of the Erie Canal and the first railroads. They were also fascinated by the prospect that steam engines, waterwheels, reapers, and other new machines would soon bring the benefits of the industrial revolution to their country.

Although Jackson had achieved fame earlier as a defender of the frontier against the Indians, the British, and the Spanish, he saw no need during his presidency to change the status quo on the frontier. One of the few times the West figured in his policy making occurred when, as part of his infamous scheme for Indian removal, he decided that the area later known as Oklahoma would be a good dumping ground for the Indians of the southern states.

Thoughtful Americans of that era viewed the expansionist policies of the British Empire in India and elsewhere with distrust and contempt. This was a legacy of two wars for independence, and it reflected the belief by citizens of a onetime colony that it was morally wrong for England and other European nations to use military force to acquire colonies and establish imperialistic regimes. The word "empire" bore negative, European connotations until Manifest Destiny propagandists dressed it in American clothes.

In the two decades that followed 1825, the national government did little to aid the initial phase of western settlement. This neglect is underscored by a glaring contradiction. The western war hawks in Congress who pitched their "Fifty-four Forty or Fight" slogan to the American people during the 1844 election had never sought funds to build forts or military outposts in the region west of the Missouri River.

The real American agents of expansion, the wagon families who broke trails in the West, did so on their own in the period leading up to the Mexican War. The national government did nothing of significance to help them. No funds were appropriated to build ferries or supply posts to ease the passage of families struggling to establish outposts in the West. Seen in this context, the windbags who gave belligerent speeches in Washington about Manifest Destiny were indolent spectators.

Congress' disinterest in western settlement was expressed by the character of the first military force sent into the Far West. Exploration, not settlement, was uppermost in the mind of the secretary of war in 1842 when he dispatched Lieutenant John C. Frémont and a small cadre of topographic engineers into the Rocky Mountains. These soldiers were sent not to escort wagon trains but to prepare a map of the well-traveled wagon road to the South Pass in Wyoming. As we have seen, it was churches, not the government of the United States, that provided the funds needed to support the westering of Jason Lee, Marcus Whitman, Henry Spalding, and the Mormons.

Manifest Destiny has long been depicted as a political movement that forced the nation's leaders to initiate action that extended the country's boundaries to the Pacific Ocean and paved the way for settlement of the West. In the same vein, Bernard De Voto historians have characterized James Polk, an inherently cautious and very lucky politician, as a bold president who made decisions that brought Texas, Oregon, California, and the intermountain West into the Union. Yet a judicious analysis of the events that forced Polk to make some important decisions ineluctably elevates the contributions of the early western settlers and lowers those of Polk.

The Annexation of Texas

As a result of initiatives by U.S. settlers, Texas was on a trajectory toward statehood well before the Manifest Destiny movement came into existence and before James Polk took his oath of office in 1845. The United States did not, as some contended, "grab" Texas to prevent Great Britain from acquiring it. The Texans who established an independent republic in 1836 were U.S. citizens who had been encouraged by Mexican officials to immigrate into a land area contiguous to the boundary of the United States.

The first president of the nascent Republic of Texas was Sam Houston, a onetime Tennessee congressman. Houston mounted a campaign for statehood soon after Texas won its war of independence in 1836. This campaign stirred controversy in Washington that continued for almost a decade. At one point Houston pretended he was seriously negotiating with a British emissary, a shrewd tactic that helped change crucial votes in Congress.

The "lame duck" Congress that convened in the winter of 1845 approved a joint annexation resolution. President John Tyler approved this document, and it was on the incoming president's desk as an item of unfinished business when Polk took office the first week in March. Polk acquiesced and sent the resolution to the Texans for appropriate action. A constitution drafted by the Texas legislature was subsequently submitted to the new Congress and approved in December.

The War with Mexico

With its empire flags flying, the doctrine of Manifest Destiny was field-tested during the war with Mexico. The outcome for both President Polk and the apostles of Manifest Destiny can best be described as a strange ride with a strange ending.

Despite intense pressure from the war hawks, a pragmatic Polk attempted to resolve existing disputes with Mexico by offering to purchase the land that loomed as a logical area for U.S. expansion. Knowing that Mexico was bankrupt, Polk sent a special emissary to Mexico City with authority to offer $5 million for New Mexico and $15 million for Upper California. The rejection of this offer influenced Polk to make the only bellicose decision of his presidency. With a maneuver he knew would ignite a war the United States could easily win, Polk ordered General Zachary Taylor to station troops on the Rio Grande as an affirmation that the United States considered it the true international boundary. With the pretext he needed when Mexican troops crossed the river, President Polk declared that American soil had been violated and submitted a declaration of war to Congress.

Considering the economic and military disparities between the two countries, the outcome of the war was foreseeable. By the end of 1846, Mexico's feeble armies in New Mexico and California had been overwhelmed and U.S. forces had gained control of these provinces. A few months later, a stalwart army of volunteers led by General Winfield Scott landed at Vera Cruz and headed inland. Led in the field by such junior officers as Captains Robert E. Lee and George B. McClellan and Lieutenant Ulysses S. Grant, by mid-September 1847 Scott's army had overwhelmed Mexican resistance and entered the storied halls of Montezuma as conquerors.

This martial feat emboldened the proponents of Manifest Destiny to demand that "by right of conquest" Congress should immediately annex all of Mexico to the Union. For the hawks, General Scott's victory was a dream come true. One editor expressed the exhilaration of his fellows when he wrote: "The whole of Mexico is upon us. It is already ours. We have it and we know it not."

This marked the high tide of Manifest Destiny jingoism, for the contentious all-Mexico debate that ensued not only roiled the politics of the upcoming presidential election but also forced Americans to confront the implications of impetuous expansion. The conservative Whigs not only were opposed to annexing Mexico but also, on principle, were against enlarging the country's boundaries by military aggression. When a no-territory-by-conquest resolution was introduced in the United States Senate, every Whig but one voted for it.

Support for the grandiose aims of the Destiny doctrinaires rapidly eroded as Americans began analyzing the perplexing questions their nation would face if Mexico were annexed outright. Would instant citizenship be conferred on Mexico's overwhelmingly Indian population? Would the United States be perceived in Europe as a militaristic, landgrabbing nation if Mexico were occupied indefinitely by American troops? Would the United States be able to absorb what Edward Everett (the former ambassador to England) described in a letter to Lord Aberdeen as Mexico's "outlandish population"? Above all, would an imperialistic stance alter the image Americans had long presented to the world as a citadel of government by the people and for the people?

As General Scott awaited instructions, it became obvious that the fervor aroused by Manifest Destiny hawks had raised grave issues about the aims and ideals of American democracy. President Polk, for example, found himself in a political whipsaw when it appeared that the annexation of Mexico would reignite the debate about slavery, divide his party, and imperil the peace won by his armies.

In an ironic twist, the president was rescued from his predicament by the audacity of Nicholas Trist, a special emissary Polk had sent to Mexico City but subsequently had fired because of supposed incompetence. Trist, with the tacit support of General Scott, had the temerity to enter into unauthorized negotiations with Mexico's leaders during the winter of 1848 in the city of Guadalupe Hidalgo. Trist had no instructions from Washington but presumed that the president would be satisfied if titles to California and New Mexico were purchased by the United States. When a courier delivered Trist's treaty to President Polk in February 1848, its terms deflated the arguments of the war hawks and created a common ground that ultimately made it an acceptable compromise. President Polk promptly submitted Trist's treaty to the Senate for ratification. It put him in a position to take credit for producing "an honorable peace" and reject the controversial all-Mexico solution. His Whig opponents treated Trist's document as a confirmation of their argument that conquest by force constituted a betrayal of the nation's heritage. This protean piece of paper also gave the Manifest Destiny agitators room to backpedal and pretend that their policy had set the stage for Mexico to enter the Union later.

Amid the all-Mexico debate, the most eloquent spokesman against the Manifest Destiny doctrine—and for the democratic values enshrined in the Declaration of Independence—was Albert Gallatin. At eighty-seven years of age, Gallatin was the last leaf on the tree of the American Revolution, and he had held high positions in the federal government under the first six presidents, culminating as secretary of the treasury under Thomas Jefferson and James Madison.

During the all-Mexico controversy, Gallatin composed a

series of articles titled "Peace with Mexico," which were framed as a rebuke to Manifest Destiny–style expansionism. Gallatin, who applauded Jefferson's policy of expansion by purchase, counseled his countrymen that in a world where most people lived under monarchies, the United States had a historic mission to be a beacon for democratic government.

Gallatin concluded one essay with this rebuke to the exponents of the Manifest Destiny hawks:

> Instead [of focusing on America's mission] an appeal has been made to your worst passions; to cupidity; to the thirst for unjust aggrandizement by brutal force; to the love of military fame and false glory; and it has even been tried to pervert the noblest feelings of your nature. The attempt is made to make you abandon the lofty position which your fathers occupied, to substitute for it the political morality and heathen patriotism of the heroes and statesmen of antiquity.

The approval of Trist's project derailed the Manifest Destiny crusade. And Albert Gallatin's appeal gained a timely resonance when historic political upheavals took place later that year in western Europe. One month after the Treaty of Guadalupe Hidalgo was ratified, a popular revolution in France ousted King Louis-Philippe. The political agitation that followed made 1848 a watershed year for democracy in Europe. Uprisings in Vienna, Berlin, Rome, Hungary, Venice, Milan, and Parma pitchforked leaders such as Giuseppe Mazzini and Lajos Kossuth onto the world stage. Those revolutions affirmed the faith of Americans that their example of constitutional democracy was still a vital force in world affairs.

Although it faded as the rallying cry of a political movement in Washington, "Manifest Destiny" enjoyed a second life as a convenient slogan for many writers and became a versatile platitude that offered simplistic explanations for complex events. By invoking this glib phrase, for example, a writer could convey the impression that the destruction of the lives and cultures of native peoples came about with the acquiescence of the Almighty. And as an exculpatory device, this imperialistic slogan had many uses. For example, it allowed chroniclers the luxury of depersonalizing history. Thus, the decimation of the buffalo and the plundering of the West's resources could be attributed not to the short-sighted greed of exploiters but to a disembodied force called Manifest Destiny. And if a writer or historian wanted to condone mistakes and giveaways by national leaders during the Gilded Age, the blame for lapses that mortgaged the West's future could be laid at the door of this same faceless force.

Down-to-earth action eventually always overshadows rhetoric, and during the two years of political hullabaloo in Washington, the future of the West was actually being shaped by settlers who were then pouring into Oregon, northern California, and Utah.

6 California Gold Fever: Fact and Fancy

"[Mining] is perhaps the most disadvantageous lottery in the world, or the one in which the gain of those who draw the prizes bears the least proportion to the loss of those who draw the blanks."

—Adam Smith

Since the beginning of human history, gold's aura has inspired myths and folktales, and the conventional story of the California gold rush fits within the classic contours of this phenomenon. Enveloped in a layer of romance that has obscured important truths, this human stampede looms as one of the most exaggerated, misinterpreted chapters of American history.

Dreams of gold occupy a special place in folklore, beginning with the mythical tale of Jason and his search for a magical Golden Fleece. According to legend, when Jason set sail in the *Argo,* he was accompanied by a band of heroes Greek writers called Argonauts, a term that came to be associated with gold seekers. Spanish conquistadores came under the spell of this dream in the sixteenth century, when, intoxicated by visions of sudden wealth, they quested for rumored cities of gold in the American Southwest.

This mania reappeared three centuries later when reports of gold strikes inspired thousands of adventurers on several continents to depart for a little-known region that had just been annexed to the United States of America. The timing of this stampede gave the California gold rush a dramatic niche in American history. It had an international impetus because it occurred when advances in maritime transportation made it possible for gold seekers to reach San Francisco from all parts of the globe. And it was distinctive because it took place in a remote, sparsely populated region that had no effective government.

The so-called prospectors who came to northern California as this scramble for personal gain got under way were a motley lot. They spoke many different languages, and most had to pick up the crude techniques of placer mining by watching early birds pan for gold in random streams. Typically self-centered to the core, most of the rushers were driven by the desire to accumulate a nest egg of gold dust or nuggets and return in triumph to their homes.

But the chaotic nature of the human stampede made it impossible for all but a lucky few to fulfill their dreams of sudden wealth: the amount of ore was finite, most of the best sites for prospecting were preempted early on, and an unprepared military government did nothing to control mining activities or provide preference rights for its citizens.

The California Gold Rush in Perspective

Facts about American gold rushes are sketchy. In California, for example, since there were no local governments and the "population" consisted of arriving and departing transients, it is difficult to ascertain who accumulated what precious metals during the first frantic years of that rush. Estimates that have found their way into history books indicate that half of the approximately 80,000 U.S. prospectors who completed the trek to northern California in 1849 traveled overland, the rest came on ships, and probably one-fourth of all gold rushers came from foreign countries.

It is difficult to trace the flow of humanity at the height of the rush. Indications are that thousands of discouraged prospectors gave up and went home in 1850, for example, and that additional hordes arrived the same year. The first hard information can be found in a special 1852 census: it revealed that California's population had swelled to 223,856, from about 25,000 prior to the rush.

Although relatively few profited from it, the output of California's goldfields was phenomenal. After the first decade of frantic surface mining, it was clear that the foothills of the Sierra Nevada contained the world's largest known deposits of gold. By 1880, statisticians have estimated, California's Mother Lode had yielded an output greater than the total tonnage of gold produced in the previous 350 years of human history.

For the nation, the glow generated by its gold rush made California a cynosure and produced a quick political reward. Although California had been part of the United States for less than three years—and had never undergone the customary tutelage as a territory—in September 1850 the United States Congress passed a law making it the first state in the Far West.

The state's first elected leaders had to deal with problems that were compounded daily as new waves of immigrants arrived. Because California had no laws, no law enforcement machinery, and no effective government to speak of, years of struggle were required to transform camp towns and rickety "cities" into orderly communities.

The instant city of San Francisco was a macrocosm of the problems California faced. Endowed with a superb natural harbor, San Francisco almost overnight was listed on the world's maps as an important maritime port. Yet, despite its many natural advantages, San Francisco qualified by the summer of 1851 as one of the most vulnerable, haphazard agglomerations of human beings on the planet. In the preceding eighteen months, for example, six major fires had swept through its ramshackle array of tents and hutches and storefronts.

That people rebuilt on yesterday's rubble says something about the tenacity of the gold rushers who had decided to stay and make a new life for themselves in the hillsides of the San Francisco Bay Area. There were no fire departments, no police, no sanitation controls, no banks, and no real government, but somehow the polyglot population periodically performed a phoenix ritual that became a hallmark of San Francisco's resilience and that found its ultimate expression much later, in the months following the great earthquake of 1906.

In the beginning it was an alliance of bold, ruthless businessmen who brought a semblance of order to San Francisco and Sacramento by hiring guards to protect their property—and by organizing vigilante groups to dole out extralegal forms of street punishment. A few merchant princes were big winners in the California gold rush, as one might expect. Some of these shrewd indigenous capitalists made millions as land speculators; others amassed wealth by importing machinery to create sawmills, ironworks, textile mills, shipyards, and factories that provided tools and goods for incoming prospectors and materials for the state's newborn cities. Take, for example, Collis P. Huntington, a onetime Connecticut traveling salesman who parlayed profits from a monopoly featuring $50 shovels and very expensive blasting powder to amass the capital that enabled him to become one of the nation's foremost railroad magnates.

Overblown claims about the effects of the California gold rush have skewed perceptions of the West's early history. The view that this stampede *changed the West*—now a centerpiece of conventional wisdom—has long conveyed the impression that this scramble became *the* defining event of western history.

The unbridled free-for-all of 1849–1851 did alter the situation in a small sector of the Far West, of course. The sudden rise of San Francisco as a city gave the United States an anchor and port for world trade on the rim of the Pacific Ocean, and it created economic opportunities that galvanized growth in the Bay Area. By the end of the 1850s, the prospect of lavish profits had persuaded a venturesome group of mining men to build wagon roads over the Sierra Nevada and to develop ways to mine the rich silver deposits that had been discovered in western Nevada. And the region's explosive growth (northern California's population was approaching 350,000 by 1860) emboldened four successful entrepreneurs to unite and begin exploring the feasibility of building a transcontinental railroad to connect their region with national markets.

Although the gold rush generated widespread change in northern California, the modifications it produced elsewhere in the West were surprisingly minimal. Two full decades were to elapse before fulfillment of the initial railroad dreams of the Big Four (Collis P. Huntington, Mark Hopkins, Charles Crocker, and Leland Stanford, California's Mexican War governor), but in the meantime, frontier families in southern California and other parts of the West moved forward, developing farms and building churches and other community facilities.

It was the advent of railroads in the 1870s and 1880s and the access they provided to the machines of the industrial age that introduced a new era of material progress in the West. What jump-started the growth of Los Angeles, Phoenix, Portland, Seattle, Butte, and other areas was new technologies. The economic takeoff of these communities occurred when energy became available from combustion engines rather than mules, when handsaws were succeeded by chain saws and big sawmills, and when modern mining equipment displaced pick-and-shovel digging.

The Big Four provided the start-up capital and arranged federal financing that ultimately led to completion of the western segment of the famous first transcontinental railroad in 1869. It was, however, Gilded Age lobbying skills rather than accumulations of gold dust that enabled these men to bring their plan for the Central Pacific Railroad (CP) to fruition. After the Civil War, schemes for new railroads went nowhere unless they were headed by promoters who knew how to wheel and deal in the corridors of power in Washington, D.C., and come away with huge federal loans and subsidies. Machinations by Collis Huntington and Governor Stanford won crucial support in the nation's capital, but anticipated labor costs for constructing a track up and over the Sierra Nevada massif confronted the manager of the CP with seemingly insurmountable difficulties.

Undaunted, Charles Crocker solved this problem by recruiting a desperately poor, subservient Chinese workforce. His agents imported more than 10,000 sturdy peasants and took them to the mountains to perform, for a pittance, the high-risk, backbreaking work needed to place tracks through seemingly impossible terrain. The herculean feats of these immigrants went unnoticed when the nation celebrated "American perseverance" in the spring of 1869 as the CP's track was joined in Utah to that of the westbound Union Pacific Railroad. This insult was compounded soon afterward when racist Californians led a national campaign to ban further immigration by Chinese citizens.

The Dark Side of the Gold Rush

Gold fever not only influenced the conduct of the feckless prospectors who rushed to California with inflated expectations.

It also intoxicated the imaginations of writers and encouraged them to romanticize the California stampede, portraying it as a daring exploit by young Americans who served the nation by opening the whole West to settlement. The myth of the California gold rush is so deeply embedded in the minds of the American people that it flourishes today as the epic adventure of the nineteenth century, with 1849 enshrined as a "year of glory" for the nation.

In recent years, New West historians have illuminated many related dark recesses of western history. To augment the work of these scholars and put the saga of the Golden State in perspective, the argument that follows focuses on five questions:

1. What effect did the California gold rush have on the lives of individual miners?
2. What effect did the rush have on California society?
3. What deleterious long-term influence did the rush have on the conservation of resources in the Golden State and the rest of the American West?
4. What effect did the gold rush have on the lives of the Indians, the Spanish settlers, the Asian immigrants, and the prospectors who emigrated from Mexico and Latin America?
5. To what extent did California's gold rush influence mineral policy in the country as a whole?

THE MINERS

Stripped of its romantic trappings, the California gold rush was a harebrained venture. The tens of thousands of young men (most in their twenties) who chose to go west were chasing a will-o'-the-wisp. Few knew anything about mining or had any realistic idea of the risks they were taking. And the rumors that aroused their imaginations provided no information about the quantities of gold that might be available or the obstacles prospectors would encounter in attempting to find some of it.

Their treks were typically self-centered ones. There was no call to action by religious or secular leaders. To be sure, some went with the hope of returning and bettering the lot of their families, but the thinking of the great mass of single men seemingly began and ended with the obsession that when they got to the goldfields they would be among the lucky ones and acquire quick wealth. Whether these deluded individuals traveled on steamers or crossed deserts to reach California, figuratively they were a ship of fools.

There is ample evidence that many forty-niners realized soon after they reached the diggings that they had almost certainly embarked on a wild-goose chase: the number of good placer sites was limited; there were far too many prospectors; and the best claims had already been taken. In her 1994 study *Precious Dust*, historian Paula Marks concluded that "ninety-nine out of a hundred men in the California placer diggings were lucky to make expenses." And Donald D. Jackson, author of *Gold Dust*, remarked that by the time northern California had absorbed a second wave of more than 80,000 aspiring miners in 1850, the overflowing camp towns in the Sierra Nevada foothills were "tatterdemalion refuges for an increasingly desperate and disgusted horde."

Despair had a corrosive effect on the lives of many miners and produced the most tragic chapters of the gold rush era. The prevailing hopelessness was reflected in the high level of violence and criminality in most mining camps and in the ferocity of random raids frustrated miners sometimes conducted against Indian villages. "Many miners fired at Indians," Jackson commented, "as readily as they would shoot a deer or a bear."

Where the pick-and-shovel prospectors were concerned, their

"poor man's rush" was brutal and short. In September 1850, a French correspondent, Etienne Derbec, reported, "The sweetest illusions are lost . . . from close at hand the gold disappears." The dreary, heartbreaking story of the great body of gold rushers who saw their dreams vanish, and who themselves vanished from history, will never be told. The state's first provisional governor, Peter Burnett, once speculated that 30 percent of the forty-niners died as a result of disease, accidents, or violence.

In any event, a splintering occurred in the movement that reflected the diverse reactions of disillusioned miners. The bulk of the miners who had come from the United States, duly chastened, straggled back to their homes. Some, though, remained in the region and became farmers, craftsmen, and laborers, and wives left behind joined them to become builders of northern California's first solid communities.

It is evident, too, that gold fever gained such a grip on the minds of several thousand rushers that they became gold rush bums. Over the next two decades, these rootless gypsies responded to rumors of placer strikes in Australia, British Columbia, Colorado, and Idaho by boarding ships or riding animals to such far-flung places.

Seen in this perspective, it is curious that these often foolhardy adventurers have been draped by so many writers in the mythic robes of Greek Argonauts and presented as heroic founders of civilization in the American West. This focus raises seminal questions about the saga of western settlement. Who, after all, were the valiant? And who, considering settlement in the region as a whole—not just in California—were the vanguard folk who established outposts of civilization in the West's most important valleys? Was it the frenetic single men who scurried across the West in pursuit of El Dorados and left ghost towns in their wake? Or were the real heroes and heroines the men and women who loaded their children and belongings in wagons and went into wild country to break ground for farms and create communities?

The crowning irony of the California stampede, as already noted, is that the big prizes were won either by merchants and real estate operators who already resided in the area or by astute newcomers who saw that they could realize bonanzas by providing food and services for incoming miners.

The Social Effects

Until the California gold rush, gradual expansion by groups of pioneer families had been the hallmark of frontiering in the United States. The classic situation saw families in search of free land pushing into the hinterland just beyond existing villages. Such movements usually involved groups bound together by kinship, religious ties, or both, a circumstance that inculcated cooperation and fostered mutual respect.

This farm-village pattern of settlement produced relatively homogeneous equal-opportunity societies that put a premium on order and social stability. As a consequence, new communities typically established strong links with local governments. Laws, country lawyers, and county officials occupied a central place in the lives of ordinary settlers. One can see the positive role the legal system played in people's lives by, for example, reading accounts of Abraham Lincoln's early years in Illinois as a prairie lawyer.

Socially, the California gold rush cut across the grain of this American experience. There was nothing small or gradual or familial or cohesive about this onrush. In two years, northern California was inundated by 200,000 strangers. Sacramento, a hamlet of four dwellings in April 1849, had become a ramshackle gathering place of 10,000 men by the end of that year, and San

Francisco expanded from 600 inhabitants in 1848 to an estimated population of 30,000 two years later. The absence of any civil government meant that several years would elapse before either of these gathering places would acquire the attributes of a functioning city.

Social progress requires shared goals that encourage individuals to work together to create stable societies. The social disaster that dominated the first phase of California's history was an outgrowth of the miner's every-man-for-himself mind-set; men wedded to a grab-and-go-home creed had little interest in building homes or the rudiments of communities.

The upshot was a scramble that exalted greed and produced squalid, disorderly communities. Early Sacramento gained notoriety as a place where public decisions were frequently made in the streets by competing groups of transients. One observer described the new capital of the Golden State as "one great cesspool of mud, offal, garbage, dead animals, and that worst of nuisances consequent on the entire absence of outhouses."

Their city's turbulent, polyglot population having arrived in a matter of months, San Franciscans who wanted a semblance of order faced overwhelming problems. It had taken St. Louis, the largest city west of the Mississippi River, eighty years of incremental expansion to become a city of 70,000 citizens. San Francisco might have had a chance to cope with some of its problems if the national government had sent troops to maintain order while a local government gradually came into existence. But no succor came from that quarter.

Much of northern California, not just San Francisco and Sacramento, was overwhelmed by all manner of social problems in the wake of the gold rush. Civilization did not gain a foothold until civic-minded citizens and churchmen asserted leadership that tempered the extreme individualism fostered by the great stampede. The rampant corruption and disorder of the 1850s prompted the state's ground-floor historian, Hubert Howe Bancroft, to describe that interval as a period of "moral, political and financial night."

ENVIRONMENTAL HAVOC

As the pick-and-shovel mining era petered out, a new mining technique was invented that prolonged surface mining for three decades. Called hydraulic mining, it was the most destructive method of extracting ore the world had ever seen.

Edward Matteson developed this technique in 1853 by using water pressure harnessed through a hose and nozzle to wash whole hillsides bearing specks of gold into pits or streams for processing. This laborsaving device evolved into a water cannon called the "Little Giant" that could slice away the slopes of a large hill in a single day. Voracious gold-mining companies built hundreds of miles of canals and viaducts to bring water to high-line reservoirs, where gravity "drops" generated the pressure needed to create massive avalanches.

These nozzles moved massive amounts of earth into pristine westward-flowing rivers of the Sierra Nevada. For every ounce of gold scavenged, tons of topsoil and gravel were deposited in nearby streams. During spring floods, rivers were clogged with debris, downstream communities were inundated with muck, and fertile farmlands were blanketed with mud and gravel.

The devastation of Marysville, once a riverside port on the Sacramento River for side-wheel steamboats, dramatized the damage caused by this monstrous machine. As mine muck filled the riverbed, home owners were forced to build levees that ultimately rose higher than their rooftops. The depredations of the hydraulic miners were unrelenting, however, and in 1875

Marysville was buried in mine wastes when a spring storm washed away the walls the town had patiently erected.

City dwellers and farmers who suffered severe damage protested, but they got nowhere. The gold rush had enshrined a value system that gave the hydraulic mining industry in California a legal right to decimate mountain valleys even if homes and farms were destroyed, rivers became impassable, and the ecology of vast tracts of forested uplands was irreparably impaired.

This value system gave gold extraction a sacrosanct status for three decades, until the California legislature finally outlawed hydraulic mining in 1884. During this interval, gravel became the gravestone of many agrarian communities and the hydraulic mining companies set a record for industrial land abuse unparalleled in the nineteenth century.

Rapacious attitudes toward land spawned by the California gold rush, combined with the hands-off policy of the federal government, not only produced unprecedented environmental degradation but also saddled northern California with a feudalistic pattern of landownership. The mind-set of big miners encouraged affluent businessmen in Sacramento and San Francisco to hire devious lawyers and acquire vast estates at cut-rate prices in parts of northern California.

Thomas Jefferson envisioned America as a society of family farmers whose sturdy self-reliance would ensure that Europe's monopolistic patterns of land control would never gain a foothold in the United States. In a letter to John Jay, U.S. secretary of foreign affairs, in 1785, Jefferson expressed his faith in the nation's yeoman farmers: "Cultivators of the earth are the most valuable citizens. They are the most vigorous, the most independent, the most virtuous, and they are tied to their country, and wedded to its liberty and interests, by the most lasting bonds."

Had he lived to witness it, Jefferson would surely have been dismayed by the California gold rush and by the subsequent land rush that locked the new state into a pattern of landownership reminiscent of Europe's. In the vanguard of this pageant was Major John Charles Frémont, the self-styled "conqueror of California." Before he rode east in 1847, a finagling Frémont signed a note for $3,000 and acquired title to the huge Mariposa Land Grant—a move that made him a millionaire three years later when outcrops of gold ore were discovered on his ranch.

California's champion landgrabbers, however, were Henry Miller and his partner, Charles Lux. With an eye on the main chance, Miller started as a butcher in 1850, and within a decade he and Lux emerged as the Golden State's biggest landowners. These aggressive immigrants acquired land titles, often by fraud, that made them grandee owners of 10 million acres in the San Joaquin River valley.

Within a decade, opportunities for family farmers had been effectively foreclosed in much of northern California by the machinations of acquisitive land sharks. Here is historian William G. Robbins' description of the outcome:

> The state's best farming land, including that deeded by the Mexican government to a few hundred owners before the conquest, was subjected to a period of frenzied speculation and eventually wound up in the hands of San Francisco and Sacramento capitalists who manipulated state and federal laws to amass huge holdings.

This orgy of landgrabbing created profound environmental and social problems that put California on a different path from the rest of the West. In other states and territories where early homestead laws and acreage restrictions in the 1903 Reclamation Act gave ordinary citizens preferential rights, incremental growth tied to family-size farms was the norm. Carey McWilliams put his finger on this anomaly when he asserted that every western state "experienced the leavening effect" of the federal government's "free or 'cheap' land policy . . . except California."

Prescient Californians were disturbed by the prospect of monopolistic ownership transforming huge sections of the Golden State into an agrarian empire dominated by a few land barons. Both H. H. Bancroft and philosopher Josiah Royce viewed the emerging land monopoly through dark glasses, and economist Henry George lamented that California was becoming "a country of plantations and estates." Events subsequently validated the warnings of these observers. The environmental and social consequences of this fiasco were pervasive, and the human injustices they fomented later became a focal point for the work of John Steinbeck and other writers and social reformers, such as Cesar Chavez.

RACISM's INDELIBLE STAINS

Vicious treatment meted out to minority groups during the gold rush set California on a path toward developing its own peculiar brand of virulent racism. The main victims of this discrimination were native peoples, Chinese immigrants, and miners from Latin American countries. Spanish-speaking prospectors who arrived from Mexico, Chile, and Peru were the first to feel the sting of ethnic hostility. Having previously worked in gold and silver mines, these miners knew how to locate and exploit promising placer sites, and they formed a solid front against Anglo efforts to jump their claims. In 1850, while the gold rush was in full swing, newcomers who coveted the claims of these industrious miners managed to persuade the fledgling state legislature to pass a prohibitive $20 per month foreign miner's tax designed to force these immigrants to abandon their diggings.

A prompt showdown took place, and the Spanish speakers

(including large numbers of native-born Californians) were driven out when the tax collectors made their rounds flanked by a large posse of armed Anglo miners. This coup alerted state officials to the prospect that anti-minority taxes might be a ready source of revenue. The upshot was that the governor and the legislature adopted a policy of imposing stiff taxes on other minority groups. Such punitive levies were so popular that between 1850 and 1870 almost one-half of the state's income was derived from an assortment of blatantly anti-Chinese taxes.

This was child's play compared with the genocidal activities of miners who invaded the homelands of northern California's aborigines and added a final, gruesome chapter to the history of relations between Indians and whites in California. Estimates are that when the first Spanish friars began their missionizing in 1769, California was populated by 300,000 peaceful Indians who lived lightly on the land and subsisted by fishing, gathering wild foods, and hunting small animals.

The coastal natives the Spaniards encountered were among the most gentle, least warlike Indians in the entire West. Early settlers such as John Sutter and James Marshall (the men who made the first gold strikes in 1848) employed Indians as laborers and found them to be friendly, diligent workers who respected the property of their employers. Prior to the California gold rush, remoteness had shielded the natives in Mother Lode country from contact with Europeans. This was fortuitous, we know, for in other parts of the Americas where human interaction was more intensive, European diseases decimated the populations of native communities.

Attitudes that led to exterminatory activities in the Mother Lode region were an expression of the grab-and-go frenzy that was the hallmark of the California gold rush. Unlike the slow-moving first-generation wagon families, who typically sought peaceful relations with the natives they encountered, aggressive prospectors viewed Indians as subhumans who could be killed with impunity. This mind-set was given an official seal of approval in 1850 when Thomas Butler King was sent to California on an inspection trip by President Zachary Taylor.

After surveying the situation in the mining camps, King decided that extinction of the natives was both desirable and inevitable. Author Donald D. Jackson informs us that "King described [the natives] in his report to the Secretary of State as 'degraded objects of filth and idleness' who were bound to disappear under the relentless pressure of the whites."

Even without such encouragement, brutish elements in mining camps who viewed the natives as wild animals conducted "Indian hunts" with the aim of wiping out all native inhabitants in raids that Bancroft characterized as butcherings. Where respect for the rights and welfare of native peoples is concerned, California presents a dismal spectacle. Alvin Josephy Jr. adjudged that the inhumane attitudes and activities generated by the California gold rush brought the natives of northern California "as close to genocide as any tribal people had faced, or would face, on the North American continent."

The slaughters and injustices of anti-native activities and the wholesale theft of Indian lands was so blatant that, in the 1880s, Helen Hunt Jackson took up her pen and denounced the attitudes and policies that had degraded and diminished California's Indian heritage. In her novel *Ramona*, she excoriated the indifference and neglect that was wiping out the culture of the Mission Indians. Harsh facts such as she presented helped spawn the 1890s cliché that the nation's aboriginal people were "vanishing Americans."

In contrast to what happened in most other areas of the West, in California the federal government (amid the hurly-burly of the gold rush) adopted a do-nothing policy where the new state's Indians were concerned. This was a fateful decision. It made dispossession the de facto Indian policy.

This default by federal officials sounded a death knell for the natives. It meant they were, in effect, wild animals who had no rights. And it meant they would have no opportunity to retain homelands where they could perpetuate their cultures. The scale of the dispossession that followed is dramatized today by the contrast between Indian landownership in California and that in Arizona. Today, Arizona's natives own 28 percent of the land area embraced by the boundaries of that state. In California, Indians own 1 percent of the land.

Next to the natives, the Chinese were the main victims of ethnic racism spawned by gold fever and the lawless attitudes it perpetuated. Most of the Chinese who came to California during the gold rush were peasant farmers. Some of them farmed small plots and provided food to sustain the stampeders; others went into the hills and worked as scavengers at placer sites other miners had abandoned.

The sporadic riots directed at Chinese communities were expressions of blind prejudice. There is no evidence that these immigrants committed violent acts or provoked confrontations by jumping the claims of other miners. In a strange, turbulent environment, they kept to themselves and achieved their modest aims by diligence and hard work. Under these circumstances, the intense animosity displayed in campaigns against the Chinese seems mindless unless one surmises that disappointed prospectors needed to feel superior to other gold rushers and vented their frustrations in attacks on passive folk who would not retaliate. What we do know is that the anti-Asian racism that reared its head during the gold rush poisoned California's social and political environment for nearly a century.

The Gigantic Mineral Giveaway

The adage "Haste makes waste" fits the California gold rush, for this stampede abruptly forced an unprepared nation to make, even if by default, far-reaching and unfortunate decisions about immensely valuable resources owned by its citizens.

The concept that the sovereign was entitled to collect a substantial "royalty" on the minerals acquired by its citizens was well established in the sixteenth century. In Spain, for example, the ruling monarch's one-fifth share was called the *quinto real* (royal fifth). Thus, when Spain's conquistadores seized the golden treasures of the Aztecs and Incas and later mined rich deposits of silver, penalties were severe if these metals were not promptly taxed and stamped by Spanish officials. Indeed, it was lavish New World revenues that enabled Spain to be Europe's military superpower and maintain the strongest economy during the epoch known as the Golden Century of Spain.

Officials of the British Empire were equally assiduous as stewards of the Crown's mineral assets. British authorities acted with dispatch in the 1850s after deposits of gold were discovered in Australia and Canada. When gold strikes were made in the Fraser River area of present-day British Columbia in 1858, for example, the British governor forestalled a California-style scramble by calling in a detachment of the Royal Canadian Mounted Police and requiring that all incoming miners pay stiff license fees and comply with the rules governing extraction of ores.

In California, the United States got off on the wrong foot— and set the stage for a gigantic giveaway of its precious minerals—when federal policy makers adopted a hands-off policy and did nothing to regulate the exploitation of this resource. No laws were passed or proposed, no soldiers were sent to preserve order, and there were no serious policy discussions in Washington concerning royalties or fees that could be collected and used to improve the lives of Americans.

With little governance at hand, in the beginning disputes about mining claims were resolved by threats or by gunfights or other acts of violence. In an effort to avoid violence, prospectors in some mining camps soon developed and posted informal ground rules for newcomers. These rules outlined steps by which miners could stake claims to specific tracts and retain their rights by scarring the earth with occasional pick-and-shovel work.

These ad hoc rules, devised to dampen conflicts between competing miners, were framed by individuals who operated on the presumption that the rest of society had no legitimate interest in the matter. These camp regulations came to be known as "the miners' code," and when the Civil War ended, California's congressmen sponsored sweeping legislation to enlarge even further the rights of prospectors. Their ultimate statute, the General Mining Act of 1872, opened all the West's public lands to prospecting. According to its provisions, by making a nominal payment, miners who staked claims and subsequently filed an application with a federal land office would, ipso facto, acquire outright ownership of all minerals embedded in their claim.

By disavowing the idea that states and the nation had a stake in the hard-rock minerals (gold, silver, lead, copper, iron, etc.) located in the West's public lands, the 1872 act was a death knell for any system of royalties or leasing fees. This law became the touchstone of a mining industry that had become an economic powerhouse in the West and mustered political muscle to fend off efforts by reformers in Congress to make miners remit royalties similar to those paid by coal and petroleum companies.

With passage of the 1872 act, California's style of grab-and-go mining was installed as the American way, producing adverse consequences for both the country as a whole and the American

West. Some mineral economists have estimated, for example, that if hard-rock mining companies had been required to pay normal royalties, sums approaching a trillion dollars would have flowed into the U.S. Treasury.

The 1872 statute is the most profligate law ever enacted by the United States Congress. The absurdity and magnitude of the annual giveaway were underscored in the late 1990s when that law forced Secretary of the Interior Bruce Babbitt to convey land in Arizona containing $2.9 billion worth of copper for a payment of just $1,745 by a foreign mining company. The open-door, come-and-get-it policy spawned by the California gold rush also set a precedent for raids on the West's timber, grassland, and wildlife resources.

Historian Vernon L. Parrington described the outcome as a "great barbecue" of the West's resources. This onslaught gained momentum during the administration of Ulysses S. Grant, when the buffalo were slaughtered and the plundering of vast forests got under way. And the rampage continued until President Theodore Roosevelt and reformers who called themselves conservationists appeared. They led campaigns that began to change the nation's values and to produce laws and concepts of land stewardship that would make wise management of resources part of the American creed.

Despite all the hyperbole attached to the California gold rush—that it served as the origin of the American dream, symbolized the courage and spirit of the pioneers, opened the West for settlement, and changed the course of United States history—the reality was far from the glamorous story promoted by the myth-makers. Even those scholars who concede that the California gold rush was a disaster for almost all prospectors are reluctant to let this dreary truth mar the mythic glow of their narratives. Gold rush writers are tempted to burnish the images of greed-driven Argonauts and to give even the failures of these adventurers a heroic spin. One author recently sentimentalized that the miners "dreamed of riches but the experience itself became the real treasure." Others, to end their accounts of the California caper on a note of triumph, tell us that "it was the quest that mattered."

Yet, with the dawn of a new century, we surely should look behind the curtain of gold rush myths and glory stories and deal with the unvarnished facts. We cannot understand our history unless we see it whole and tell it true.

7 Bootstrap Capitalism in the Old West

*T*he California gold rush, as we have seen, was not a catalyst that significantly altered the pace of development in the West as a whole. On the one hand, there was already appreciable homesteading and town building in many parts of the West; on the other, the general modernization and economic transformation associated with infusions of outside capital did not begin until railroads provided service to various regions of the West.

To appreciate the calendar of the American West's development, then, it is important to recognize these basic realities: that the West was not a quiescent outback in the pre-railroad era; that animals, not steam engines, provided most of the energy settlers needed for commerce and travel; and that outside investments did not begin to flow to inland regions until rail lines provided connections with eastern markets.

It is a gross distortion of history to assume that little of economic significance happened until investments by eastern capitalists brought technologies of the industrial age into the region. The agrarian pioneers were not a collection of backward-looking clodhoppers. Once their farms provided adequate food and fiber, they concentrated on improvements that would enable them to produce surpluses and find markets for their commodities.

Where the Old West is concerned, historians now recognize

that the genesis of American capitalism took place in pastoral settings. The late George Ellsworth, a keen student of western trends, made this point while observing that agriculture is "the most fundamental of all human activities." Once "the agricultural surplus essential to civilized life was produced," he noted, western farmers began creating "small footholds of civilization . . . in an otherwise forbidding land."

Such footholds were enlarged on the frontier by energetic settlers who established social and political institutions that prepared the way for economic advances. Wagon pioneers made assiduous efforts to improve the production of essential goods and to import machines that could serve community needs. They purchased equipment such as sawmills, gristmills, and paper mills, using "prairie schooners" to transport them to their towns and villages. Combining the skills of their blacksmiths, carpenters, masons, sawyers, and other artisans, they built bridges, schools, dams, canals, and other facilities needed to enhance the functioning of their communities.

In organizing these efforts, Protestant, Catholic, and Mormon communities used a similar approach, tapping the savings of their parishioners to buy machines and materials and marshaling workforces for particular projects. Well before the venture capitalists moved into the West, many communities were enjoying the benefits provided by a sturdy infrastructure of chapels, schools, hospitals, and other amenities. The social values that made such projects feasible constituted a counterpoint to the coming conventional creed of capitalism. The "capital" each individual invested was hard work, and no one made much of a monetary profit. The palpable outcome, however, was that everyone profited when the quality of community life was enhanced.

The impression conveyed by some historians that nothing of

real significance happened until eastern investors began industrializing parts of the West disregards other of the many accomplishments of the first-wave pioneers as well. Before the railroads came, freight wagon commerce thrived on the Santa Fe Trail, for example, while New Mexico's Catholics created an architectural landmark with their construction of the first Gothic chapel in the Far West. And the spacious Mormon Tabernacle, built by Mormon craftsmen between 1864 and 1867 and featuring a ceiling supported by hand-hewn beams and wooden pegs, was a structure that won recognition for having the largest unsupported arch in the world.

Even in remote areas, efforts in the pre-railroad period produced advances that paved the way for future economic growth. For example, to extend the reach of agriculture in the arid provinces of the intermountain West, farmers banded together to construct small reservoirs and irrigation canals, and nascent communities organized volunteer work crews to build bridges, jails, courthouses, and schools.

Thrifty local folk also pooled their savings and found outlets to engage in manifold forms of what can be called bootstrap capitalism. Some opened stores, operated ferries, or provided other needed services. Others loaded their wagons with lumber or foodstuffs and traveled long distances to sell their surpluses in mining camps in Idaho, Montana, Colorado, and Nevada.

Work my grandfather, David K. Udall, did as a teenager in the late 1860s illustrates the efforts some farm families made to take their produce to distant markets. The winter David was sixteen, he worked for a contractor in Weber Canyon, pushing gravel in a wheelbarrow to build the grade for the Union Pacific Railroad. He used his savings to buy a yoke of steers he named Pat and Roy, and in each of four subsequent winters he harnessed his Pat and Roy to a wagon loaded with flour and grain to sell and made

First home of David K. Udall in
St. Johns, Arizona, ca. 1880

a 500-mile round-trip from Nephi, Utah, to the silver-mining town of Pioche, Nevada.

Although it is true that capital from many countries poured into northern California in the 1850s, the 1880 census underscores the extent to which San Francisco and its environs was what Allan Nevins once described as "a world unto itself." California, the census tallies showed, was 38 percent urbanized at a time when five territories (Dakota, Idaho, Montana, Washington, and Wyoming) had no city with a population of more than 5,000 inhabitants—and only Omaha, Denver, and Salt Lake City boasted populations of more than 20,000 citizens.

Almost overnight, San Francisco in the 1850s became an emporium of capitalism. Maritime access for steamships, a superb natural harbor, and an ideal location for the only major North American port on the Pacific Rim made San Francisco a magnet for international commerce. In a few years, such advantages combined with explosive economic growth in the Bay Area

The West in 1880

The 1880 U.S. census reveals that the West was still predominantly a rural region of ranches, farm villages, and small towns.

State/Territory	Total Population
Arizona	40,440
California	864,694
Colorado	194,327
Dakota	135,777
Idaho	32,610
Kansas	996,096
Montana	39,159
Nebraska	452,402
Nevada	62,266
New Mexico	119,565
Oregon	174,768
Utah	143,963
Washington	75,116
Wyoming	20,789

Salient 1880 Facts

- Five territories (Dakota, Idaho, Montana, Washington, and Wyoming) did not have a city of 5,000 or more citizens.
- Except for Oakland, Sacramento, and San Francisco in northern California, the only western cities with substantial populations were Denver (35,629), Omaha (30,518), and Salt Lake City (20,678). All these cities were served by railroads.
- The largest town in Montana was Helena (3,624), and the largest in Washington was Walla Walla (3,588).
- Los Angeles boasted a population of 11,183.
- Tucson led Arizona with 7,007 residents, Boise topped Idaho with 1,899, and Santa Fe led New Mexico with 6,635.
- Portland led Oregon with 17,577 residents.
- Butte, Montana, was a small camp of prospectors staking out silver claims. The same year, the silver-mining boomtown of Leadville, Colorado, had 14,850 residents.

to enable local entrepreneurs to establish manufacturing plants, which a British visitor compared to those he had seen in Philadelphia and Liverpool.

In the three decades that followed the discovery of gold at Sutter's Mill, however, opportunities for California businessmen to hasten economic development in the rest of the West were circumscribed. Steamships generated coastal trade with small ports in the Oregon Country, but possibilities for inland commerce were limited by the existence of that rugged natural barrier known as the Sierra Nevada. Before the first transcontinental trains arrived in 1869, the only way to penetrate this daunting terrain was with pack mules and teams pulling freight wagons.

Before 1869, there was only one instance in which California capitalists made a significant investment in the hinterland beyond the state's boundaries. This transpired in 1859, when rich veins of ore containing three-fourths pure silver and one-fourth gold were found at what became Nevada's fabled Comstock Lode. That discovery persuaded George Hearst and a few other venturesome San Franciscans to assemble enough capital to purchase and transport heavy machinery to the site, where engineers activated stamp mills and created the first extensive underground mining operation in the American West.

Considering constraints that limited the reach of California's capitalists, it is surprising that the idea persists that the California gold rush changed the West. It was not even success stories of California prospectors, but another epidemic of gold fever, that produced later rushes to remote inland areas. In 1859, swarms of prospectors invaded Colorado; smaller stampedes took place in 1860 to Idaho and in 1862 to Montana. The quantities of placer gold obtained in these instances were piddling compared with the Mother Lode, and these rushes resulted mainly in small-scale repetitions of the social chaos and personal tragedies that characterized the California rush.

These second-wave Argonauts, like their California forerunners, evinced little interest in building communities. Prospectors' self-centered aims were underscored in the summer of 1859 by the harebrained "Pikes Peak or Bust" gold rush. The Pikes Peak rush reveals how a mirage fashioned by rumors could deprive men of their common sense as it set in motion a mindless migration that was the antithesis of real settlement. In this case, false reports of huge gold strikes had persuaded 100,000 easterners to head toward patches of wild country in the Rocky Mountains. Half of these hopefuls turned back before they reached the Colorado diggings, and by the end of the year slim pickings had busted the dreams of late-coming Argonauts huddled in scabrous mining camps. When the 1860 census was taken the following spring, the largest nonurban "community" in the new territory of Colorado was a ramshackle camp named South Park, and life in the quickie city named Denver was controlled by a professional gambler.

The same boom-and-bust outcome characterized the influx of prospectors into the mountain valleys of Idaho and Montana in the ensuing few years. There is little evidence to support assertions that these raids changed the West in positive ways. Historian Keith L. Bryant sardonically noted that "it would be hard to exaggerate the rootlessness of the miners and their followers." In a similar vein, Richard White quotes a novelist who called the storied boomtown of Leadville, Colorado, "a senseless, rootless place," and Allan Nevins once characterized this kind of mining as a "jerky, wasteful and, in striking degree, an evanescent development, without much direct profit to the territories involved."

These rushes did create short-term markets for energetic agrarians. When pack animals sold at premium prices, stockmen reaped handsome rewards. And amid frantic demands for food and construction materials, enterprising farmers profited by loading their wagons with flour, lumber, beef, dried fruit, and other foodstuffs and driving long distances to mining camps. One of the striking ironies of western history is that while volatile mining ventures waxed and waned in self-styled "mining states" such as Colorado, Idaho, Utah, and Nevada, year in and year out the varied enterprises of agrarians remained those areas' real economic mainstay.

The Old West Time Line

With the emplacement of railroad trunk lines, it suddenly became feasible to import the latest technologies of the industrial revolution, which induced venture capitalists of the Gilded Age to cast covetous eyes on the region's rich mineral and forest resources. In *Colony and Empire: The Capitalist Transformation of the American West*, William G. Robbins provided a useful frame of reference for analyzing the upshot of this investment interest when he observed that "in reality, the Guggenheims and the Goulds, the Harrimans and the Hearsts, and the Morgans and Mellons heavily influenced what the West was to become." By focusing on the chronology of activities of Robbins' six capitalists, one can fix with some precision when outside investments ushered different regions of the West into the nation's economic mainstream.

The Guggenheims made their debut as western investors in the late 1870s, when they purchased an interest in silver mines in Leadville, Colorado. Success there led to other ventures that enabled them to establish dominance in the mining and smelting of copper in the 1890s. Western resources first aroused Jay Gould's speculative fervor in the early 1880s, when, along with Andrew Mellon, he invested in a mining venture in the Coeur d'Alene district of northern Idaho. During this same period, Gould, Edward H. Harriman, J. P. Morgan, and the Guggenheims provided capital for the construction of four trunk lines that would link their mines in Sonora and Chihuahua with U.S. rail centers along the Mexican border.

As noted earlier, George Hearst was not really a global capitalist but a bold western gambler who specialized in indigenous investments. Ever the opportunist, in the mid-1870s Hearst took swift action when he learned that federal troops were allowing prospectors to invade the Black Hills homeland of the Sioux. His aggressive agents acquired mining claims that became the famed Homestake Mine, which holds the record for gold output in the United States. Later, Hearst founded a San Francisco syndicate that staked out surface silver claims in Butte, Montana, which later digging disclosed were located on the apex of the world's richest lode of copper.

Although such investments quickened economic activity and introduced changes that began altering lives and living conditions in some areas of the West, it is important to keep the overall realities in perspective. The 1880 census reveals that the West was still preponderantly an agrarian region of villages and small towns: 83 percent of westerners then lived in rural environments. Northern California was rather an anomaly: population there exceeded the total number of inhabitants residing in Arizona, Dakota, Idaho, Montana, Nevada, New Mexico, Oregon, Utah, Washington, and Wyoming.

Dramatic transformations produced by the railroads were most evident first in southern California and in the Pacific Northwest. Los Angeles, known as the "Queen of the Cow Counties" in the 1850s, was a sprawling agricultural area of 11,000 citizens in 1880. Spurred by one-dollar train fares from midwestern cities, the flow of immigrants into southern California was so great that the population of Los Angeles increased fivefold in the following five years. A similar great leap occurred in Washington Territory after the Northern Pacific Railway completed its track to Tacoma in 1883. The avalanche of immigrants who arrived aboard trains galvanized urbanization in Portland, Seattle, Tacoma, and Spokane and swelled the population of Washington from 75,000 in 1880 to 357,000 only a decade later.

Similarly, steam-engine transportation spurred steady, but less spectacular, growth in Phoenix, Tucson, Albuquerque, San Diego, and Salt Lake City as rail access enabled those cities to serve as hubs of commerce for their hinterlands. This development replicated what had happened earlier in Kansas and Nebraska when train transportation encouraged homesteading and accelerated the expansion of communities such as Topeka, Wichita, Omaha, and Lincoln.

Except for the towns they created to serve as way stations for their enterprises, railway companies, out of necessity, had to interact with settlers and the communities already established in western valleys. As a result, greedy business decisions (such as excessive shipping rates) made by railroad magnates had an immediate and often adverse effect on the lives of the customers and communities they served. This evoked grassroots protests against price fixing and other abuses and forced Congress to pass laws in the late 1880s that curtailed the power of the nation's railroads and limited their capacity to dominate the lives and politics of ordinary people.

As supposed transformers of the region's culture, the global capitalists in charge when the western mining industry got under way in the 1880s were a special case. Single-minded to a fault, they sent their capital and their mine managers into the West not to change social conditions but to extract ores by whatever methods would yield maximum profits.

Nature dictated that the West's richest mineral deposits would be located in rugged, remote environments. As a result, mining companies starting from scratch had to build feeder tracks to mainline railroads, bring in heavy mining machinery, and create makeshift communities for their workers. Large-scale industrial mining gave birth to a new mode of western settlement wherein absentee mine owners established self-contained "company towns" ruled by managers who had auto-cratic power.

The managerial model adopted by the mining magnates was patterned after strategies that had enabled Andrew Carnegie and John D. Rockefeller to create giant steel and oil trusts and amass huge fortunes. Carnegie and Rockefeller were efficient, ruthless operators who won monopolies over markets by driving com-petitors to the brink of bankruptcy and acquiring their assets at bargain prices. They also attained economic dominance by installing the latest and best machines and processes in their own plants, which typically enabled them to outcompete their rivals in productivity. But the capstone of their industrial plan was a pay-as-little-as-possible (PALAP) wage policy, which all but guaran-teed that their investments would generate lavish profits.

Under the federal government's giveaway resource policies, the managers sent into the field by the mining moguls to set up their enterprises had an array of economic advantages Carnegie and Rockefeller, in their offices in Pittsburgh and Cleveland, surely envied:

- They paid trifles for the gold, silver, and copper ores they extracted.
- They could harvest wood they needed for construction and to fire their smelters free of royalty charge by clear-cutting nearby forests.
- They could acquire the land required for mill sites and town-sites for a pittance.

In frontier locations out of national view, hard-rock mining in the West became a tightfisted, control-oriented industry. In the initial towns established by these owners, the industrial plant and the houses, stores, saloons, bordellos, and streets were owned by the corporation, and company police were on hand to convert the decisions of the mine managers into local "laws" and rules that governed conduct in those secluded enclaves. The bonuses these businessmen enjoyed were huge: plenary control put the companies in a position to recapture a large portion of the wages paid to their employees, and their political power gave them leverage that minimized interference by state and territorial governments.

In settings where absolute power prevailed, it was simple to implement hiring policies that allowed a PALAP wage strategy to flourish. The companies usually hired experienced Cornish or Irish miners as foremen and sent agents to impoverished eastern European countries to recruit and provide passage money for husky, illiterate laborers who would ask few questions about the perils lurking in underground mines.

In the early years of the company towns, this system produced another bonanza: the bulk of the miners were young emigrants from semi-feudal societies who were willing to work for the wages offered by "benefactors" who helped them immigrate to America. In Utah's mining history, Italians and Slavs came first, followed by Greek miners when agents of Leonidas Skliris, an affluent Salt Lake City businessman known as the "Czar of the Greeks," made it possible for large numbers of his countrymen to flock to the Beehive State. Different ethnic mixes were assembled in other mining regions. Arizona's location near the border, for example, produced an inflow of Mexican miners who became a large, pliant component of the workforce in that territory.

During the 1880s, the gaze of eastern investors in the West rarely strayed from their balance sheets. These were not broad-gauged, magnanimous individuals who identified with the impulses then animating Andrew Carnegie's philanthropic work. Rather, they were obsessed with the prospect of quickly recouping their initial investments and amassing larger fortunes. The corporations they headed spent little on amenities to improve the lives of their employees—and few of the owners took overt steps to improve the quality of life in the company towns and nascent states where they were doing business.

Poet Archibald MacLeish provided a literary snapshot of the mind-set of these big capitalists in his verse "Wildwest":

> It was all prices to them: they never looked at it:
> why should they look at the land? they were
> Empire builders: it was all in the bid and the
> asked and the ink on their books. . . .

Butte: The Great Exception

Some have argued that the frontier environment made a profit-obsessed company town outcome inevitable in mining areas. Montana scholar and social historian David Emmons, however, challenges this contention in *The Butte Irish: Class and Ethnicity in an American Mining Town, 1875–1925,* surely one of the most illuminating books written in recent decades about social aspects of western history.

Emmons uses Butte's history to demonstrate that there was in fact a democratic, communitarian alternative to company town mining. Butte, he shows, was the outgrowth of "a set of social values at variance with those of acquisitive capitalism." If more owners had shown an interest in social betterment, he suggests, mining towns could have rivaled the achievements of the West's agrarian folk in building stable, cohesive communities.

In Emmons' view, a vital element of Butte's success involved the story of Irish immigrant families working together to create a cohesive community. Butte in the nineteenth century was "everything the West was not supposed to be: intensely urban, massively industrialized, overwhelmingly immigrant and Catholic."

Butte occupies a special place in mining history because it sits on what has been called the richest hill on Earth. "In population, production and size of work force," Emmons notes, "it had no rivals among the mining cities anywhere in the world." Beginning in 1882, Butte's miners were paid $3.50 for a nine-hour shift, the highest wage in industrial America at the time. The town enjoyed long-term peace and prosperity: it had the nation's most effective labor union and a pact between its employers and workers that lasted for thirty-six years, enabling Butte to avoid the turbulent disputes that for more than half a century made hardrock mining a brutal industrial battleground in the West.

Butte did not evolve into a conventional company town because it had the good fortune at the outset to fall under the guidance of Marcus Daly, an unorthodox but masterful mine manager. An Irishman himself, Daly immigrated to San Francisco in the 1860s, then worked underground in a Comstock silver mine, and later became a foreman and manager of small mines in Nevada and Utah. He was sent to Butte in 1876 at the age of thirty-five to determine the potential of some silver claims, which he and his partners subsequently purchased.

As a mining man who learned the business from the bottom up, Daly developed an uncanny capacity to make good predictions about the potential of ore bodies. In 1880 he used some of his savings to buy the Anaconda, a producing mine twenty miles west of Butte with a modest output of silver ore. When excavation revealed that the mine was located on a rich deposit of copper, Daly developed a bold but tenuous scheme to build not just a smelter but a city, on the assumption that the country would need huge supplies of copper in the future.

Daly got the capital he needed for this risky project from George Hearst and his San Francisco partners Lloyd Tevis and James Ben Ali Haggin. Daly converted the Anaconda into a copper mine, acquired title to surrounding mining claims, built a modern smelter, and was finishing work on the new Montana city of Anaconda when the first train of the Northern Pacific Railway chugged into Butte in 1883.

Daly took another big gamble when he sat down with the leaders of the new Butte Miners' Union and agreed to pay its members unprecedented wages. He never explained the impulse that encouraged him to experiment with a pay scale that made his workers "aristocrats of American labor." Having himself started as a raw immigrant who experienced the dangers in underground stopes, Daly surely understood the outlook of young miners and may have reasoned that the best way to ensure a steady flow of profits for his investors was to have a well-paid, contented workforce.

Unlike so many of his counterparts, Daly did not develop an autocratic outlook. His style was that of "one of the boys"; he attended mass as an ordinary parishioner and joined the local chapter of the Ancient Order of Hibernians. He "was more driven by dreams of building something indestructible than in amassing money," Emmons surmises. And knowing full well that men were being maimed and their lives shortened in the mine shafts, Daly apparently wanted to share some of his financial success with his Irish brothers.

Whatever his motives and pro–Irish Catholic proclivities may have been, Daly's decisions made Butte a family-oriented community. According to Emmons, the glue that held together this gathering of immigrants was that "the Irish ran everything . . . the labor union, the town, *and* the company."

Daly's Butte proved there was an attractive alternative to the conventional company town managed so as to swell the balance sheets of absentee owners. He and his partners also demonstrated that astute westerners could develop profitable mines without infusions of eastern capital. And, most notably, Daly's share-the-profits formula not only set a pay standard for the West but also served as a rebuke to the Rockefellers and Carnegies in the East who maximized their take by minimizing the wages paid to their workers.

There is a fascinating communitarian overlap between the mine-oriented society created by Butte's Irish Catholics and the agrarian communities created by Utah's Mormons. This in large measure could be attributable to the commonality of values and beliefs instilled in the minds of the faithful by their churches.

The Mormons and the Butte Irish shared a yen for large families, a commitment to an organized ingathering of immigrants, and a view that the welfare of the community deserved precedence over self-centered plans of individuals. Both cultures, in addition, tended to be clannish in social and business affairs, and both adhered to a family-first conservatism that evoked generosity when bereft members of a congregation needed help. In these respects, one could say of some Mormon communities what Emmons says about Butte: that it should be viewed as "an antidote to the historical myth of a Protestant, rural West."

The trouble with big bang interpretations of western history—that backward, semi-stagnant societies were transformed by gold rushes or dramatic infusions of global capital—is that they depersonalize the overall story of settlement and are based on assumptions that oversimplify what actually transpired. Social and cultural development in the American West was not a sudden trombone fanfare but a symphony featuring muted communal contributions by the entire orchestra.

The day-by-day efforts of settlers who were, in the felicitous phrase of social historian Janet Finn, "crafting the everyday" to improve the quality of life in their communities prepared the way for the era of modernization that began in most areas in the 1880s. Likewise, the joint efforts of people—and the projects they completed using indigenous forms of bootstrap capitalism—produced societies that were ready to cope with the transitions made feasible when railroad transportation became available.

History has been shortchanged by writers who use a fast-forward approach to blur the seminal contributions of the early settlers, whose deeds laid the foundations for the social, political, and cultural development of the West.

III Violence in the Old West: Correcting the Record

8 The Wild West and the Wrenching of the American Chronicle

"Despite all of the mythologizing, violent fatalities in the Old West tended to be rare rather than common."
—Robert R. Dykstra

*H*ow wild was the West? One cannot put western violence into perspective without recognizing that, where firearms were concerned, there was a huge difference between the primitive weapons available in the Old West of the wagon settlers and the firepower of the guns civilians owned after the Civil War. In his great memoir, General Ulysses S. Grant observed that during the battles of the Mexican War, "at a distance of a few hundred yards a man might fire at you all day long without your finding out." The killing power of six-guns and rapid-fire rifles, which were not developed until the Civil War, along with increased social frictions that fostered lawless behavior, produced a much higher level of overall civilian violence in the postwar era than had existed previously in the West. How wild the West was depends on which West we are talking about—before or after the Civil War.

Violence and Nonviolence in the Old West

Impulses of self-preservation encouraged the lightly armed wagon families of the pre–Civil War era to use restraint in their encounters with Indians and other travelers on overland trails. These groups did not venture into the wild country as conquerors. They traveled as cautious companions who, first and last, wanted to avoid risks that would disrupt their journey to valleys where they hoped to arrive in time to plant crops and establish their homes.

Although the gold seekers' aims were starkly divergent from those of early pioneers bent on settlement, the hordes of single men bound for California's goldfields also had a selfish interest in avoiding delays. In their frantic race against time and one another, the forty-niners saw conflicts with Indians or with agrarian immigrants as distractions that could fatally delay their success in the goldfields.

The primitive weapons available in the antebellum period also contributed to the relative safety of travel on the first transcontinental trails. The immigrants wisely avoided conflicts with natives because the weapons most of them carried were cumbersome, hard to reload, single-shot hunting rifles. Lacking guns, Indian groups were constrained by the knowledge that their arrows, spears, and clubs could prevail only when they outnumbered or surprised their adversaries.

The spirit of caution induced by these realities produced a pattern of wary, sometimes even friendly, relations alongside most trails that prompted historian John D. Unruh Jr. to characterize the pre–Civil War period as a time of "essential safety" for travel. In his landmark study of overland migration, Unruh effectively undermined the legend that prewar westward migration was stained by high levels of violence between Indians and migrants. "The fatal trail confrontations that did occur were usually prompted by emigrant insults and disdain for Indian rights," Unruh pointed out, as we saw in chapter 3, concluding that the dangers of overland travel were "misrepresented by myth-makers' emphasis on Indian treachery."

During the two decades preceding the Civil War, the number of natives killed by immigrants (363, or an average of 18 per year) was comparable to the number of immigrants killed by natives (426, or an average of 21 per year). It was disease, not violence, that accounted for nine out of ten deaths on the trail. The results of his survey caused Unruh to doubt whether the mortality rate of the trails "much exceeded the average death rate among Americans resisting the call of the frontier to remain at home."

Such facts contradict the myth that prewar immigrants faced constant threats from armed Indian warriors. The responsibility for such persistent confusion rests with the legion of embellishers—beginning with William "Buffalo Bill" Cody's extravagant Wild West shows—who created the impression that post–Civil War firearms were not only available in earlier decades but also used with little provocation.

If a sharp line is drawn between these two distinctive periods—before and after the Civil War and the advent of the transcontinental railroads—we can see that most of the attacks on wagon trains took place *after* the war and that most forays by native warriors occurred on well-beaten commercial roads such as the Santa Fe Trail. The Winchester repeating rifle—the weapon that supposedly "won the West"—was not readily available until the early 1870s, and not until 1871 were metallic cartridge six-shooters first issued to U.S. soldiers. It is also revealing that nearly all the town marshals and outlaws who became American "legends" were only teenagers in the 1850s.

To present such facts is not to argue that the 1840s and 1850s were a pacific period in western history. Indeed, some violent episodes occurred even as civilization was catching up with the frontier. Although most of the prewar contacts between migrants and Plains Indians proved peaceful, in some areas deadly skirmishes erupted as settlers encroached on core areas of Indian homelands.

When natives and overlanders met trailside for the first time, their relations were not often strained by hostile attitudes. Nevertheless, the Old West lives on in the popular imagination as a turbulent, brawling region dominated by gunfighters, outlaws, Indian wars, and devil-may-care gold rushers. Acknowledging the power of these images, historian Richard White commented that most Americans are convinced that "the 19th century west was a perpetually violent and lawless place."

Technological developments in the aftermath of the Civil War both altered and ameliorated the economic and social conditions of western settlement. Most changes promoted order, but a few increased conflicts between individuals and groups. Railroads were the paramount agent of change, and they influenced the course of change in myriad ways. Although it took promoters nearly three decades to complete lines into all the main regions, significant development commenced as soon as tracks were extended westward from St. Paul, Omaha, Kansas City, and Fort Worth and delivered incoming migrants into unplowed heartlands.

Not only did new railheads provide access to national markets; machines they transported made the benefits of the rapidly evolving industrial age available to fledgling communities. And the prospect that branch lines could be built into remote areas encouraged eastern capitalists to contemplate bringing heavy machinery into wilderness settings and creating boomtowns in locations where minerals and lumber could be extracted and shipped to markets.

Along with acknowledgment of the great importance of railroads, the impression is often conveyed that nothing significant happened in western transportation in the pre-railroad period. But such interpretations ignore the use of waterways and the feats of wagon masters who harnessed the energy of horses, mules, and oxen. By the late 1850s, overland stages were carrying passengers and mail between the Mississippi River valley and San Francisco, and freighting companies on the Missouri River were shipping goods and machines brought upriver on steamboats to inland towns.

At the same time, settlers in the intermountain territories were using the energy of draft animals to transport produce over long distances to regional markets. Enterprising farmers, for example, used caravans of heavy wagons to deliver goods that sustained early mining camps in Montana, Idaho, Nevada, and Colorado. And all during the 1860s, the Mormons sent "church trains" to the Missouri River valley to bring thousands of European converts and cargoes of capital goods to Utah. What railroads did, then, was increase the intensity of this traffic and reach into areas where transport had previously been difficult.

Violence after the Civil War

"Personal violence certainly could reach extraordinary levels in the West, but it remained confined to very narrow social milieus."
—Richard White

In the postwar period, disputes over land boundaries and grazing rights generated some deadly—though typically short-lived—conflicts in some regions of the West. In most instances, these were quarrels between individuals or families. The local clashes that resulted in the most casualties involved conflicts between mega-ranchers and small stockmen over free grass and water on unclaimed public lands. On a larger scale, the most violent disputes arose when the buffalo were exterminated and U.S. soldiers forced the Plains Indians from their traditional hunting grounds.

In most sections of the West, stockmen resolved range conflicts by compromise. However, in a few areas—notably central Texas—cattlemen armed their ranch-hands and disputes over property boundaries were resolved by ambushes or exchanges of gunfire. Thanks to pulp-fiction writers, some of these events entered the portals of western history as "wars."

Wyoming was another state where turf fights among cattlemen dominated a phase of its history. The open-range era in Wyoming began after the Sioux were defeated and affluent "British gentlemen" and other outside investors came west and assembled huge herds of cattle that grazed free of charge on millions of acres of public land. In short order, the Wyoming Stock Growers Association controlled the state government, and the governor trumpeted that the cattle business was "the most profitable business in the world."

In the freewheeling open-range environment that emerged, it was inevitable that deadly disputes would arise between large cattle outfits and small homesteaders. In 1891, for example, some of Wyoming's grandee ranchers hired twenty-two Texas gunmen and sent them to Johnson County to kill or "clean out" nesters (homesteaders) resisting the inroads of their herds. This incursion attracted national attention when the homesteaders fought back and captured the invading "army."

In the 1870s and 1880s, there were also homicidal disputes over grazing rights in Montana, in one Arizona county, in two New Mexico counties, and in two areas of western Nebraska. But unlike the case in Wyoming, these confrontations were local and had minimal effect on the social and political history of those states.

Certain feuds in Arizona and New Mexico have been sensationalized as "wars" by writers and magnified into events of lasting historical significance. Arizona's famous Tonto Basin War in the 1880s was actually a protracted old-fashioned feud between two families. This private quarrel produced a sequence of retaliatory ambush killings in a remote part of the state. The general public and the local sheriff learned little about the course of the feud. Yet, despite a sparsity of eyewitness accounts, author Earle Forrest won readers decades later by incorporating elements of drama in retelling the events and titling his book *Arizona's Dark and Bloody Ground.*

New Mexico's even more notorious feud gained notoriety as the Lincoln County War. In truth, it was nothing more than a series of shoot-outs between cowboys hired by competing mercantile companies in a thinly populated area 200 miles south of Santa Fe. The feud resulted in a few deaths but had no effect whatsoever on the lives of ordinary folk in the rest of the state.

Thanks to legends fashioned by filmmakers, boomtowns and the myths featuring Wyatt Earp and his fellow travelers have entered Hollywood's Elysian fields as a defining metaphor of western history for most Americans. To be sure, there were isolated violence-prone boomtowns in the Old West, but these quickie communities were atypical of western towns. Many of them mushroomed in secluded places, but even there gunplay was episodic and short-lived.

This truth applies with equal force to Dodge City and the famous cow towns of Kansas and to the early mining towns that flourished for a season or two in mountainous parts of the West. The most violent places were magnets for footloose single men who fought boredom with copious quantities of liquor. Order arrived late in the boomtowns, where there were few jails and more than half the businesses were saloons.

Outlaws such as William Bonney (originally Henry Bonney or possibly Henry McCarty)—more popularly known as Billy the Kid—typically lived and died in the outback and were rescued from oblivion by writers of pulp fiction. No aspect of western history has been so inflated and overdramatized as the activities of these legendary figures. Those who insist that robbers such as Jesse James were widely admired in some circles as American Robin Hoods too easily ignore the high value attached to law and order in communities where the great bulk of westerners resided.

Western history has been demeaned and distorted by writers who insinuate that the region as a whole suffered through "renegade years" and aver that the streets of some towns flowed with blood nightly. Such interpretations ignore the fact that outlaws laid low most of the time and focused their raids not on struggling, cash-poor villages but on larger communities with thriving banks and mercantile establishments.

Conventional accounts of the Old West's vigilance committees also need critical scrutiny. Profound differences emerge when one analyzes the motives of the disparate groups that marched under the vigilante banner. Some, led by prominent community leaders, encompassed well-meaning efforts to establish a semblance of order. Others were made up of ignorant individuals motivated by racial or ethnic animosities who sought to kill or subjugate those who they believed posed threats to their economic interests; still other committees appeared more or less spontaneously in response to local homicides. Formed in anger, the vigilance committees were usually headed by prominent citizens who took the law into their own hands. They apprehended individuals who were thought to have committed a capital crime, conducted peremptory trials, and carried out their verdicts by hanging. Many forays by these proponents of street justice involved murders in which evidence of wrongdoing was strong and law enforcement institutions were weak or nonexistent. In most instances, only one or two individuals were captured and condemned.

Favorable publicity about discipline imposed by two early citizen posses lent respectability to such activities. In 1851, a vigilance campaign led by prominent San Francisco businessmen produced a public event wherein four miscreants were hanged and twenty other putative lawbreakers were put on ships bound for foreign ports. In 1864, during a single month in Montana, outraged vigilance committees hanged twenty-five suspected "road agents" who had preyed on miners in the goldfields near Virginia City.

The mobs that killed and oppressed members of minority groups in some parts of the West were driven by baser motives. The organizers of these homicidal forays were not seeking to curb criminal activities. They wanted to crush the livelihood and the rights of "foreigners" and outcast groups. In northern California's Round Valley, for example, raiding parties of white men killed natives and expelled them from their homelands. Later, in Los Angeles, Seattle, and Tacoma, deadly riots were mounted against Chinese immigrants by agitators who coveted their jobs and businesses. Perhaps the most devastating of these pogroms occurred in Rock Springs, Wyoming, when fifty-one Chinese coal miners were massacred and several hundred were forced to flee.

But the most abhorrent use of deadly force by civilians in the postwar period was a prolonged private lynching party operating in the Missouri Breaks area of Montana. This hunt for supposed wrongdoers cannot be described as a vigilante movement, for it was not a response to local criminal activity. Rather, it was organized by grandees of Montana's cattle industry with the aim of wiping out small ranchers and farmers, who, they contended, were stealing their horses and cattle.

The expedition was organized by Granville Stuart, a cattle baron who put more than 100 "nesters" and small ranchers on a death list. Stuart's two-year effort began in 1882, at the end of Montana's frontier era. Montana was not a raw frontier when this killing spree occurred; it was already linked to eastern cities by a railroad, Butte was booming as the nation's new copper capital, and the state boasted a penitentiary and a respectable system of justice.

With lordly contempt for the law, Stuart and the cattle kings met secretly, created a code of punishment for their "kingdom," decreed the theft of a horse or calf a capital offense, and ordered their hired hands to hang the individuals they had blacklisted and burn their homes. The serial lynchings, performed by marauders who called themselves "Stuart's Stranglers," should, of course, have been greeted with abhorrence but instead were presented to Montanans as a triumph that brought law and order to their commonwealth. When Montana gained statehood a few years later, Stuart was even lionized as a noble founder, and the foul deeds of his men were later commemorated by murals in the new capitol.

An analysis of civilian violence yields these insights about the postwar West:

• If areas where considerable personal violence occurred are plotted on a map, they appear as mere pimples. Social historian Robert R. Dykstra not only lamented "the evolution of the sturdy pioneer into the Marlboro Man" but also commented that the overwhelming number of communities in the postwar West were probably as law-abiding as similar towns in the farm states of the Midwest.

- Instances of personal violence waxed where social controls were weak or nonexistent and waned as soon as communities enacted laws and hired officers to enforce them.
- Human impulses toward violence were tempered in towns where mutual cooperation was traditional and face-to-face contacts were a feature of everyday life.
- Disorder was anathema to agrarians trying to wrest a living from the land and to frontier businessmen, who needed stable social conditions to prosper.

Religious faith was the sheet anchor in most frontier towns. Whether one studies the lives of Bohemian settlers in Nebraska, Scandinavian Lutherans in the Dakotas, Mennonites in Kansas, Germans in western Texas, Mormons in Utah, Spanish Catholics in New Mexico, Presbyterians in Oregon, or the Irish immigrants who poured into Butte, Montana, it becomes clear that amity was prized and churchmen usually succeeded in dampening frictions or resolving disputes in their communities.

The Military Atrocities

If a comprehensive history of western violence is ever written, it must include not simply the personal and civilian violence just described but also the goriest chapter of all, atrocities committed against the native peoples by units of the U.S. Army during its vaunted conquest of the West.

Atrocities perpetrated during the Civil War foreshadowed subsequent events in Indian country. The worst of these mass killings were carried out by glory-seeking western officers who felt deprived of an opportunity to win battle stars in the big war in the East. One such worthy was Colonel Patrick Connor, whose assigned mission was to keep a lid on the so-called Mormon Rebellion. Connor, restless in Salt Lake City, ventured forth in 1863 with his troops, attacked a Shoshone village on Idaho's Bear River, and slaughtered 240 women, children, and old men.

Another glory seeker was a Colorado militia leader, Colonel John Chivington. In 1864, his troops ambushed a peaceful winter camp of Cheyenne families on Colorado's Sand Creek. Chivington triumphantly returned to Denver with scalps and boasted that he had killed 500 hostile Indians. A third wartime "hero" of this ilk was General James H. Carleton, stationed in Santa Fe. On a hunch that gold would be discovered on the Navajo reservation, Carleton sent his soldiers to round up and remove all Navajos from their ancestral homes. The general's starve-them-out campaign culminated in a deadly 400-mile winter march for the Navajos across New Mexico in 1864 to a bleak new reservation on the Pecos River.

After the surrender of the Confederate forces at Appomattox, opportunities to forge humane Indian policies appeared when churchmen who were sickened by accounts of atrocities briefly gained influence in Washington, D.C. These opportunities were squandered, however, when men of goodwill sent to negotiate agreements with native groups were not given the authority, the funds, or the manpower to devise and implement realistic peace plans.

The failure of this "Quaker policy" and the inept performance of officials of the Grant administration thrust decision making into the hands of William Tecumseh Sherman and Philip Sheridan, two officers whose unrelenting campaigns had shortened the Civil War. When recalcitrant Indians ignored orders issued by Sherman and Sheridan, it was inevitable that the generals would view the West's "Indian problem" as an issue to be resolved by military force.

As field commander, General Sheridan required decisive victories. Consequently, when bands of hunting Indians won skirmishes with his troops, he decided to "make war on the families" by encouraging efforts to wipe out the great herds of buffalo that sustained their nomadic way of life. He told the Texas legislature that the buffalo-hunters were doing more than his troops to subjugate the Plains Indians. The military commanders in charge of the campaign to subjugate the Plains Indians loudly proclaimed that the surest way to subdue them was to slaughter the buffalo.

General Sheridan's kill-and-destroy strategy produced one military atrocity after another. The first took place on the Washita River in the winter of 1868, when a cavalry unit—led by none other than George Armstrong Custer—surrounded and attacked a village of sleeping Cheyenne Indians located within the boundaries of a designated sanctuary called Indian Territory. In a matter of minutes, Custer's unit massacred 140 natives, half of whom were women and children.

Another especially grisly midwinter massacre occurred two years later on the Marias River in northern Montana when Sheridan sent a cavalry unit to punish recalcitrant Blackfoot Indians. The victims this time were a defenseless Blackfoot band crippled by a smallpox epidemic. Weeks later, the Board of Indian Commissioners identified the victims as 90 women, 50 children under the age of ten, and a cohort of fewer than 30 sickly "fighting men." General Sheridan's tactics led ineluctably to the infamous "battle" at Wounded Knee, South Dakota, and its record list of Indian deaths.

In the process of glorifying individual gunfights, the mythologists who created the Wild West legends chose to view such military excesses as an integral and necessary part of the march of conquest that "tamed" the West for civilization. This exculpatory outlook (characterized as "patriotic gore" by Edmund Wilson) warped history in two ways. It gave writers license to treat the massacres of natives as a necessary evil, and it made gunfighters, outlaws, and vigilantes synonymous with western violence.

The militarization of American thinking during the Civil War years generated additional distortions. When the victory parades ended and the army was sent west to "subdue the savages," Sheridan, Sherman, and other winning generals had become national heroes and the victories were associated with combat between battalions. The upshot was that even brief, fitful encounters with Indian bands that yielded few casualties were reported in the press as "battles" or "wars."

One offspring of this hyperbole became the cliché of western history known as the "Great Sioux War" of 1876–1877. This appellation, which probably originated in the feverish mind of a journalist or an aide to an ambitious general, became a hitching post for most historians. But to call this military exercise "great" is inane, and to classify the year-long pursuit and roundup of Sioux hunters and their families as a "war" debases every rational explanation of that term.

A real war involves a martial quarrel between nations or armed groups whose fighting men are assembled for direct combat; unless the adversaries want an armed contest, however, a deadly fight does not ensue. It is clear that in the final week of June 1876, the Sioux hunting parties on the Little Bighorn River were not seeking a showdown with the U.S. Army. The famous, fateful fight of June 25 was provoked by General Custer's headlong attack on a peaceful encampment of six bands of buffalo Indians. This was a surprise raid by mounted troops, not a planned test of strength by contending armies, and it was an encounter that had disastrous consequences for both sides.

The army suffered a catastrophe when Custer and his entire complement of 179 soldiers were wiped out. Historian Robert M. Utley explained why the Sioux defenders prevailed:

They won because they outnumbered the enemy three to one; because they were united, confident, and angry; and above all because the immediate threat to their women and children fired every man with determination to save his family.

It was a classic Pyrrhic victory. By humiliating the U.S. Army, the Sioux unleashed a martial whirlwind that brought defeat and despair. In the ten months that followed, cavalrymen prevailed because they enjoyed overwhelming advantages in manpower, firepower, and midwinter staying power. The supposed Great Sioux War was not a battle but a systematic pursuit of starving hunting families, who were ultimately hounded into submission or driven into sanctuaries in Canada.

Those who persist in describing the chases that occurred after the Custer massacre as "battles" trivialize history by placing these mismatched skirmishes alongside the battles fought at Gettysburg and Antietam in America's military pantheon. The scale and importance of encounters in the Great Sioux War—like the descriptions of fights with native peoples in other parts of the West—were routinely magnified to cast a patriotic glow over the actions, sometimes reprehensible ones, of mundane military patrols.

It is time to put the so-called Indian wars in a larger perspective. The argument that western settlement was made possible by postwar military conquests is overdrawn. The peaceful settlement of virgin river valleys was well under way before the end of the Civil War.

It was settlers, not soldiers, whose physical and political spadework laid foundations for functioning societies in the territories. Robert Utley summarized the big picture with these words: "The real conquerors were the pioneers who tramped westward by the thousands and then millions. . . . Undermanned and weakly led, the regular army had struggled through to the close of the Indian wars unaware that it was more a police force than a little army."

Such a perspective raises questions about the assumption that since the essence of war is violence, it follows that massacres of natives in the West by army forces were justified. This rationale has influenced latter-day students of western violence to treat frontier military atrocities as inevitable events and to exclude them from their chronologies—an outlook that allows them to make violence by lawless civilians a major theme of western history while viewing military massacres as a separate, unrelated subject.

The absurdity of this assumption is dramatized by the facts surrounding the Battle of Wounded Knee, the army's bloody thrust that crushed the Ghost Dance ceremonies of Sioux Indians. The stage for this tragedy was set in the late 1880s when defeated, demoralized natives were drawn to the millennial message of Wovoka, a Paiute messiah who first appeared in Nevada. Viewed as a Christlike figure, Wovoka preached a brand of pacifism. "Do no harm to anyone," he said; "do right always." He assured his followers that if they adhered to his Ghost Dance religion, they would ascend into space and later be set down among the ghosts of their ancestors in a new world inhabited by Indians.

Wovoka's message appealed to the downtrodden Sioux, and Ghost Dance ceremonies were performed in the Dakotas. Even though there were no manifestations of violence, the Pine Ridge Indian agent reacted hysterically to the dancers' fervor and sent frantic appeals for military intervention. In his Chicago headquarters, a politically ambitious "Indian fighter," General Nelson Miles, responded by sending troops to the area with orders that the Ghost Dance leaders and their followers be arrested and imprisoned.

Miles' decision set the stage for a Christmas week tragedy. The dancers who were surrounded and disarmed in subzero weather numbered 120 men and 230 women and children. When one native fired a rifle he had hidden, hand-to-hand fighting broke out. Amid this melee, army gunners on a nearby hill strafed the encampment using their Hotchkiss guns and killed or wounded two-thirds of the Indians.

The realities surrounding this massacre were never explained to the American people. Instead, impetuous decisions that brought fervent Indians and excitable soldiers into an explosive face-to-face confrontation were defended as a measured response to previous Indian atrocities. Wounded Knee lives in infamy as an example of excessive, inexcusable violence. No one has ever answered the following questions:

- What caused the military commanders to assume that natives engaged in a religious ceremony threatened the safety of other Americans?
- What influenced these same commanders to regard a man on his deathbed, the Sioux chief Big Foot, as a dangerous troublemaker?
- Who decided that the scene of an outdoor dance dedicated to worship should be characterized as "a theater of war"?
- Why did the officers in charge fail to realize that the fasting Ghost Dancers were exhausted and that their crusade, as elsewhere in the West, would soon collapse?
- Why was an order issued to arrest and confine a large group of natives when there had been no overt act of violence?

Following the pattern of his predecessors in the Great Sioux War, General Miles covered up this final Great Plains atrocity by announcing a great victory and by honoring several officers and soldiers with the Medal of Honor, the nation's highest commendation for valor.

The Battle of Wounded Knee stands today as a monument to martial excesses that stained the history of the American West. It is also a reminder that the death lists produced by celebrated gunfighters and outlaws pale when compared with the casualties inflicted on native peoples by units of the U.S. Army.

The Wild West Masquerade

For more than a century, writers, artists, and film writers fashioned a mishmash of myths that came together in the form of the Wild West, an image implanted in modern memory as the exciting story of American westering. Overwhelmed by the legends of these mythmakers, the settling of the Old West slouched into history as a dramatic story of Indians attacking wagon trains and heroic U.S. cavalrymen coming to the rescue, excited gold rushers and gunslinging outlaws, and fearless sheriffs bringing order to lawless towns.

The Wild West avalanche began in 1883 when William Cody, a consummate showman who called himself Buffalo Bill, mounted a cowboys-and-Indians road show that lasted for three decades and drew huge audiences in the American East and in Europe. The pageants Cody presented were so simple and dramatic that they became the prism through which millions of Americans viewed this receding chapter of their history.

Born in 1846, Cody spent his boyhood on a farm in Iowa during the period when the treks of the wagon pioneers were cresting. Cody's theatrical career as a western Everyman was launched in 1869 when Edward Z. C. Judson, a greenhorn pulp-fiction writer who used the pseudonym Ned Buntline, encountered him in Nebraska, listened to his braggadocio, and wrote "Buffalo Bill, The King of Border Men" for a New York magazine.

Attired in flamboyant frontier costumes, Cody drifted east to convert his celebrity status into cash. His colorful tales and his talents as a thespian attracted backers. They helped him craft melodramas for New York audiences based on his purported exploits as an Indian fighter. Encouraged by what he learned in the theatrical world, on returning to Nebraska Cody staged cow-boys-and-Indians pageants for local celebrations. These were so successful that he thought a touring company would be a hit in eastern cities.

Using the same techniques that made P. T. Barnum the mas-ter impresario of the nineteenth century, Bill Cody acquired investors, and in the summer of 1883 he reserved a special train and put his first Wild West show on the road. Advertised on gaudy posters as "America's National Entertainment," his vaude-ville acts drew huge crowds in open-air arenas.

The performances featured tableaus of horsemanship, glimpses of native cultures, and a shooting exhibition that made markswoman Annie Oakley a household name. The finale, head-lined as a scene in which "Howling Savages Pursue a Defenseless Stage Coach," was a mock battle in which an attack of blood-thirsty Indians was thwarted by rough-riding cowboys armed with six-guns.

As an impresario, Cody excelled as a casting director. Some of the Indians he recruited had participated in the famous fight with Custer, and he insisted they carry their weapons and don their warbonnets. To demonstrate that the savages truly had been subdued, in 1885 Buffalo Bill hired Sitting Bull to join his tour in full regalia. The legendary Sioux war chief rode in the parades on a beautiful gray horse and held court in a tipi, where he signed autographs for awestruck visitors.

As a promoter, "Colonel" Cody did not miss a trick. To bur-nish his fame, he hired a ghostwriter, who produced a flow of 121

"Buffalo Bill novels" that kept him in the limelight as a symbol of the fading frontier. His popularity and profits inspired imitation, and at one point more than fifty competing traveling shows were crisscrossing the country. By changing his scenarios, Cody kept his circuslike variety shows on the road for more than three decades. His pageants instilled a simple, vivid message: the West was a region where violence was an everyday experience, where hostile savages resisted the advance of pioneers, where guns prevailed over arrows and spears, and where the empire of the United States of America was enlarged by the feats of fearless cavalrymen.

With an assist from Owen Wister and Zane Grey, two extremely popular eastern novelists, by the time Cody's last show closed in 1917 his theatrical extravaganzas were accepted as the true story of western settlement. As historian Anne M. Butler reminds us, Bill Cody became "the national caretaker for western authenticity [and] almost single-handedly pushed [his] western notions into the modern scenario and made them accessible to the general public."

The whites-versus-Indians battles staged by Buffalo Bill involved fights between faceless groups. The novels of Wister and Grey provided a face—a gunfighting, justice-seeking cowboy—and a simple plot that evolved into the western, the twentieth century's most successful film formula. Moviemakers subsequently molded their protagonist into a heroic figure whose deeds made it possible to bring civilization into the American West.

Wister was a Philadelphia lawyer who spent a few summers on Wyoming ranches in the closing days of the frontier era. Grey, a young dentist from upstate New York, was so enchanted when he first saw the West in 1905 that he moved there. He became the most widely read author of his generation—15 million copies of his cowboy romances were purchased by avid readers. The works of Wister and Grey made meager contributions to American literature, but the scenarios in the fictions became cornerstones of the emerging edifice known as the Wild West.

As literary heirs of the Buffalo Bill tradition, Wister and Grey exhibited little interest in the experiences of actual settlers. The quiet struggles of men and women building homes, farms, and communities in frontier settings did not appeal to their imaginations. Needing exciting action to sell their books, they portrayed the West as a male bastion of badmen, skulking Indians, and fearless cowboys whose guns protected the lives and property of their neighbors.

Wild West stories and characters were made to order for the entrepreneurs who flocked to Hollywood to develop moving pictures that would appeal to mass audiences. Scenarios featuring cowboys, horses, and guns were a natural for the first generation of filmmakers. Thus, it was no accident that Hollywood's first identifiable star would be William S. Hart, a stern, taciturn, straight-shooting cowboy. The theatrical sons of Bill Hart—progeny running a gamut from director John Ford to actor Clint Eastwood—created a genre that became a distinctive feature of American culture. Their gaudy images captured a masquerade of legends that obscured the real West.

A raft of fascinating questions are raised by the psychological process by which this new form of entertainment produced such a result. How, for example, did fictions presented to mass audiences win acceptance as capsules of actual history? Why did westerns, with their stereotyped plots and foreseeable endings, mesmerize Americans for decades? Did myths about western settlement eclipse facts in viewers' minds because the virtues and moral triumphs of the cowboy heroes were so satisfying? Or did other influences, such as the West's stunning landscapes, combine to infiltrate Wild West values and themes into the main-stream of the nation's culture?

Explanations may vary, but in reality the phenomenal appeal of westerns—and the brainwashing accomplished by their myths—was widened with the advent of television. For much of the 1950s, eight out of ten prime-time television shows were seri-alized westerns based on variations of the Wyatt Earp "epic," and Hollywood's studios were grinding out a new cowboy movie almost every week. This mythmaking caper was put in perspec-tive by William Kittredge, head of the University of Montana's creative writing program, when he described it as "art designed for the widest possible audience, all of America and the world overseas, and as such it isn't about anybody really, and it's not centered anywhere actual."

After a half-century of screenings, the clichés depicted in westerns had acquired such authenticity that theaters became de facto classrooms where celluloid legends were transformed into historical facts. Only a few western historians challenged Holly-wood's mythmakers, and they found themselves spitting into stiff breezes whipped up by Hollywood's wind machines. Here is Larry McMurtry's description of the barrier these debunkers faced: "The romance of the West is so powerful you can't really swim against the current. Whatever truth about the West is printed, the legend is always more potent."

When Robert Dykstra presented the findings of his meticu-lous study of violence in the West to a Sun Valley symposium titled "Western Movies: Myths and Images," Henry King, direc-tor of a "classic" western, *The Gunfighter,* delighted the audience by rebuking "the professor" and denigrating his facts. Efforts by historians to put western violence in perspective encountered opposition not only from moviemakers but also from members of their own profession who glorified gunfighters as seminal figures of western history.

Epilogue

Wild West myths have obscured the overall story of western settlement. Nearly a century elapsed, for example, after the last of the Indian "wars" before artists and writers began presenting the Indian version of their encounters with the invading whites. This turning point came with the publication of Alvin Josephy Jr.'s *The Patriot Chiefs* (1961), Vine Deloria Jr.'s *Custer Died for Your Sins* (1969), and Dee Brown's *Bury My Heart at Wounded Knee* (1971) and the presentation of the first "pro-Indian" American film, *Little Big Man* (1970).

Had the images of the ersatz West not been so deeply implanted in the minds of Americans, an awakening might have been brought about by the words of children of pioneers—writers such as Willa Cather, Ole Rölvaag, Mari Sandoz, John Steinbeck, Wallace Stegner, and A. B. Guthrie—who created evocative accounts of the everyday lives of actual settlers that, in effect, accuse the filmmakers and their minions of hijacking western history.

One does not find routine accounts of gunfights or scenes of Main Street violence in the works of these artists. Willa Cather set a tone for these authors in her stories of the everyday lives of Nebraska farm families in *O Pioneers!* (1913) and *My Ántonia* (1918). Rölvaag struck a similar note in his novel *Giants in the Earth* (1927), which depicts the triumphs and travails of Norwegian immigrant farmers on the plains of the Dakotas. However, the voices of these writers were whisperings amid the ongoing cascade of dreamworks called westerns.

The most reliable and evocative facts about the real West can be found in the records and reminiscences of settlers. The mythmakers have inflated the significance of a few dramatic episodes, but the skin of western history is manifest in the artless letters, diaries, and journals of men and women who were actors in this epic. In recent decades, social historians have been enlarging the story of settlement by means of books and articles based on documents bequeathed by pioneer families to state historical societies and university libraries.

Details in letters written to relatives back home often combine to produce mosaics of the experiences of families and communities. Collectively, such communications constitute authentic folklore that deflates the balloons of Wild West writers. The reports of fatalities that recur in these letters typically concern not victims of gun violence but accounts of the quiet violence inflicted on communities by drought and disease, which sometimes decimated whole families.

Another balloon-deflator can be seen in the proceedings of such organizations as the Oregon Pioneer Association and the Society of California Pioneers. The annual gatherings of these settlers were dedicated to preserving respect for the achievements of the wagon pioneers. Their meetings rarely focused on Indian fights or altercations with outlaws but instead highlighted the experiences of emigrants who ventured across daunting terrain to create homes in virgin lands. Speakers recounted the trail days of Trekkers and the spirit of cooperation that enabled groups of emigrants to overcome obstacles that arose on their journeys.

More often than not, the reminiscences and the candid letters written to home folk concentrate on the communal sharing and caring that flourished on the trails and afterward. These pioneers did not see themselves as conquerors of the West, and one finds no trace of Manifest Destiny arrogance in their narratives. Listen to the summation offered by Montana's William Kittredge:

> If you start reading around in the journals and diaries and letters from the early West, mostly written by women, you will find quite a different story from those written for publication in the East. For instance, you will hardly ever find a holy gunfighter come from the wilderness to right the troubles of society.

The guileless testimony pioneers proffered to posterity provides an irreplaceable baseline of facts for those who want an accurate picture of the saga of western settlement. If this backdrop is kept in place, it debunks, all by itself, the simplistic stories that have been the stock-in-trade of the Wild West mythologists and their followers.

9   The Wild West and the Settlers: Contrasting Visions

"I firmly believe that the Western frontier was a far more civilized, more peaceful, and safer place than American society is today."
—W. Eugene Hollon

*H*aving spent most of eighty years as a citizen, public official, and writer in the American Southwest, I have had an opportunity to delve deeply beneath the legends into the actual history of my region. One can see in the descriptions of this area some dramatic instances of the process by which wayward entertainment industries have smudged and submerged the actual story of settlement. Comparisons of the treatment of Wyatt Earp and Brigham Young in Arizona and of Billy the Kid and Archbishop John Baptist Lamy in New Mexico illustrate particularly well how the peaceful, often enduring achievements of pioneers were overshadowed during the twentieth century by overblown accounts of lawless conduct. They also reveal how random incidents of violent behavior by individuals were transformed into defining events of the history of an entire region, to the detriment of our long-term understanding of American history.

Arizona: Wyatt Earp and Brigham Young

Few legends have a stronger grip on the American imagination than those surrounding Wyatt Earp. The real-life Wyatt Earp lived in Tombstone, Arizona, from 1878 until the spring of 1882 and was employed there as the city's marshal until he fled to Colorado to avoid prosecution for several ambush murders. Before his death in Los Angeles in 1929, Earp was worried that the "true story" of his life would never be told. His yearning for redemption was fulfilled with a flourish two years later when a fictionalized biography, *Wyatt Earp, Frontier Marshal,* written by a second-rate Hollywood scriptwriter named Stuart Lake, was published in New York and serialized in the *Saturday Evening Post.*

Lake's Earp was a clean-cut, fearless figure, and his book inspired a generation of film directors. It cast Tombstone as the West's typical frontier community, and its invented dialogues, evil outlaws, and dramatic shoot-outs became staples of the genre. Earp, redeemed in spades, ultimately emerged after his death as the nation's most admired frontier hero. The saga of Earp in Tombstone was lofted into American folklore in the 1950s when a wildly popular television series ran for six years in prime time and spawned rival westerns on the other networks.

In his book, Lake proclaimed that Earp deserved recognition "more than any other man of record of his time" as a leader who "laid the foundations of western empire." In the absence of a scrap of evidence that Earp made any significant contribution at all to their state's system of justice or tradition of fair play, Arizonans familiar with their region's history have viewed Lake's encomium as a Hollywood joke.

Those best qualified to pass judgment on the foundations Wyatt Earp did or did not lay in Arizona during his sojourn in Tombstone are, of course, the region's senior historians of the period. Here are their assessments:

- Lawrence Clark Powell, in his authoritative *Arizona: A Bicentennial History*, makes no reference to Wyatt Earp.
- Odie B. Faulk decided that the storied gunfight at the OK Corral was the outgrowth of a feud. In his *Arizona: A Short History*, he describes the bloody aftermath: "The public sympathized with the Clantons, and several shots were fired from ambush at the Earps and their followers. Before the Earps could be brought to trial, they fled to Colorado after shooting more of the Clanton gang, some in the back from ambush. The Earps were never extradited or made to pay for their crimes."
- In his 1982 opus *Arizona: Historic Land*, Bert Fireman summarizes his study of the pertinent documents by concluding that Billy Clanton and the McLaury brothers were unarmed at the famous corral "when they were assaulted by the Earp brothers and Doc Holliday, erstwhile gamblers and pimps who had been recruited as town officers in an ongoing political battle that was a cover-up for a stage robbery."
- Thomas Sheridan devotes eight pages to the Tombstone silver boom in *Arizona: A History*, but Wyatt Earp does not appear as a participant in the life of that community. Sheridan merely offers, in passing, the opinion that Earp "and his brothers found more than they bargained for in Tombstone."

Thanks to Hollywood's dream machine, however, Wyatt Earp has given Arizona top billing in the Wild West sweepstakes. During one of his campaigns for the presidency of the United States, Pat Buchanan sought to please the National Rifle Association, and remind Arizona voters of their distinctive status, by winding up his campaign waving a gun in Tombstone, attired in a frontier costume.

But where historical judgment is concerned, it is important to consider what was going on not just in Tombstone but also in the rest of Arizona from 1878 to 1882. For example, during this period three railroads that connected Arizona to the rest of the country were under construction or had already been completed. This interval also witnessed implementation of Brigham Young's plan to establish agrarian colonies in Arizona's Salt, Gila, and Little Colorado River valleys.

The completion of the Southern Pacific Railroad from California across Arizona to El Paso provided the territory's residents a link with the rest of the country and with the western coast of Mexico. In the same period, the Atlantic & Pacific Railroad Company completed its route from the Rio Grande across northern Arizona to California. These enterprises created railroad towns that served hinterland communities, and by the time New Mexico and Arizona achieved statehood in 1912, they were engines of economic growth that had transformed Phoenix, Tucson, and Albuquerque into the dominant cities of the desert Southwest.

Brigham Young's plan to develop homesteads in Arizona river valleys came to a climax between 1878 and 1882. The goal of Mormons was to create close-knit communities surrounded by irrigated subsistence farms. One company settled along the Salt River near present-day Mesa. Another located homesteads along benchlands of the Gila River between Solomonville and Fort Thomas, and a third created a town at St. David, on the San Pedro River, thirty miles from Tombstone. In addition, pioneers sent to northern Arizona established more than twenty farm communities on the watershed of the Little Colorado River.

Life was not easy for the farmers, who had to harness the flows of erratic rivers to water their croplands. Using axes, shovels, and primitive horse-drawn "scrapers," they carried out trial-and-error irrigation experiments, erecting rude diversion dams in streambeds and digging ditches to carry captured water to gardens and fields. In this field of activity, Woodruff, a village on the Little Colorado near Holbrook, deserves the prize for civic perseverance: between 1878 and 1919, Woodruff residents built thirteen earthen dams, of which eleven were lost to floods and one was cut voluntarily before a durable structure was emplaced.

Mormon settlers were counseled to put down roots in isolated areas and to avoid violent confrontations in their relations with Indians and other citizens. This policy emanated from an awareness that federal laws made polygamy a felony and that non-Mormon neighbors might demand that offenders be prosecuted. Thus, Mormons were encouraged to avoid disputes that could lead to gunfights. When the Apache chief Victorio led a livestock raid on Mormon villages in the White Mountains, for example, according to historian Charles S. Peterson, a policy of appeasement "averted bloodshed, though nearly every horse in the region was sooner or later taken."

Mention of these facts is not intended to depict Arizona Mormons as particularly saintly but rather to dramatize how the Wyatt Earp approach to history has distorted or overshadowed the realities of everyday life on that frontier. Bert Fireman put his finger on the intrinsic truth when (in the peroration of a speech he called "Mostly Sweat") he railed against the glorification of frontier violence and declared, "The West was won by toil, by shovels, not guns."

As the 1880s began, the great bulk of Arizonans were living in farm villages, military posts, new railroad towns, or stable cities such as Prescott and Tucson. As the brief Tombstone boom was ending, Tucson, a predominantly Catholic community, was emerging as a model of modernization for the territory. Father J. B. Salpointe, sent from Santa Fe in 1866 by Bishop Lamy, was by 1882 a bustling vicar apostolic whose parishioners were building new chapels and who was himself actively widening the reach of his church's missionizing.

Under Salpointe's aegis, the Sisters of Saint Joseph of Carondelet were busy adding new cultural dimensions to Tucson's life. These tireless nuns had made history in 1870 by founding Arizona's first academy for girls, and three years later they revived a school for Papago Indians at the Mission San Xavier del Bac. The sisters also established a hospital—the first nonmilitary medical facility in the territory—to serve the people of Tucson.

Arizona was never a violence-ridden backwater. It had a tiny population and a landlocked agrarian economy before the railroads arrived, connecting the territory with eastern markets and allowing large-scale cattle and copper enterprises to develop. Arizona's first frontier folk needed, and created, a semblance of order so that their settlement and rudimentary businesses would be protected. In his brief, violent sojourn in Arizona, Wyatt Earp contributed nothing to this important transformation.

New Mexico: Billy the Kid and Archbishop Lamy

Wyatt Earp and Billy the Kid (William Bonney) were contemporaries who never met, but there were striking similarities between their lives, both the real and the fictionalized:

- Both men made a short appearance on the southwestern stage: the murderous episodes that made them notorious took place over a period of months, not years. The Spanish saying *Pasó por aquí* (roughly, "He passed by") would be a fitting epitaph for both of them.
- Neither man had any moral compunction about killing innocent men—and there is no real evidence that either developed exceptional gunfighting skills.
- Both men lived away from mainstream locations, and the lasting effects of their activities, outside of folklore, were nil.

- Both deserved ignominy, but after their deaths (Billy's in 1881; Earp's, at age eighty-two, in 1929), both fell into the hands of writers who turned their lives into mythical stories that made them Wild West icons.

The history of America's westering suggests that there are times and seasons that are particularly conducive to the creation of larger-than-life figures to romanticize specific eras. Skillful writers, for example, transformed Daniel Boone and Davy Crockett into folk heroes whose lives became symbols of the American advance into undiscovered country. Wyatt Earp and Billy the Kid came onto the stage after the Civil War, when settlement was already well under way and pulp-fiction writers in New York were looking for action stories to use as plots for their dime novels. Cowboys and outlaws with new six-shooter handguns provided just the actors they needed for their stories.

At the time he was ambushed by a sheriff in the spring of 1881, Billy the Kid was an ordinary wrangler who had distinguished himself by shooting two unarmed deputies and escaping from jail. As biographer Robert M. Utley observed, had it not been for the extravagant stories written after his death by Marshall Ashmun Upson, the Kid "might well have vanished into oblivion."

Born in Connecticut, Upson was a well-educated wanderer who drifted into the hamlet of Roswell, New Mexico, and served as its postmaster during the Kid's last days. His storytelling gift had slumbered for fifty years, but Ash Upson sensed that he could transform the grubby life and violent death of a local outlaw into a drama that might appeal to easterners hungry for western adventure stories.

The first prose threads that were subsequently woven into the tapestry of the Billy the Kid legend were written soon after word of the young outlaw's demise reached the outside world. The *Police Gazette* informed readers about the death, and soon thereafter energetic pulp-fiction writers who had never been west of the Hudson River began composing dime-novel stories about the Kid's exploits. In less than a year, five lurid "biographies" of Billy the Kid had appeared.

The legend acquired a new dimension in 1882 with the publication of a book ghostwritten by Ash Upson for Sheriff Pat Garrett. This volume bore the flamboyant title *The Authentic Life of Billy, the Kid, the Noted Desperado of the Southwest, Whose Deeds of Daring and Blood Made His Name a Terror in New Mexico, Arizona, and Northern Mexico.* Two parts fiction and one part fact, this tome carried such authority that, as Robert M. Utley concluded, it "became implanted in the hundreds of [so-called] histories that followed."

The hoary myth was renewed and expanded in 1926 when a Chicago journalist, Walter Noble Burns, presented the young bandit as an American Robin Hood in *The Saga of Billy the Kid.* Burns' book was a best-seller, with the result that the legend excited the imaginations of Hollywood's moguls and generated an output of more than forty films that made the Kid a paramount symbol of the American West.

Hollywood's Kid was a fearless shootist whose exploits won him a reputation as a "top gun" and attracted a following of young gunslingers. This Kid, a leader in what pulp-fiction folk grandiosely referred to as the Lincoln County War, sought face-to-face confrontations with his enemies and by age twenty-one had killed twenty-one men. In the last year of his life, the Kid of legend was finally captured and convicted of a killing he had committed in self-defense. A few days before he was to be hung, he made his dramatic escape after taking the lives of two deputy sheriffs. A few weeks later, Sheriff Garrett violated the mythical "code of the West" by setting up a nighttime ambush and killing the Kid at close range with a single shot.

Once the fantasies of Upson and his ilk are separated from verifiable facts, the outline of William Bonney's life reveals a likable drifter rather than a "matchless desperado" who terrorized the Southwest. These facts intimate that young Bonney was an ordinary cowboy who had average gun skills. The real Billy was apparently a follower, not a leader, during the feud between two cattle outfits that erupted into a deadly two-day gun battle in 1878 in the tiny town of Lincoln, New Mexico. Other evidence indicates that this hardened youth killed four men, not the twenty-one touted by his mythmakers.

It is worth noting that in his Pulitzer Prize–winning biography of Archbishop Lamy, Paul Horgan devoted only a single paragraph in a book of 523 pages to the feud that erupted in Lincoln County, and he described Bonney as simply "a youthful murderer."

Juxtaposing the lives of William Bonney and Archbishop J. B. Lamy in the years 1878–1881 graphically demonstrates how mythmaking can distort a region's history. Today, if New Mexico history is mentioned, the name of Billy the Kid springs into the minds of most Americans. Embellished for more than a century by melodramatic writers and filmmakers, his legend has conveyed a message that order was maintained by gunfighting lawmen and that ordinary citizens brandished rifles and revolvers wherever they went.

Yet this precise time period also witnessed a culmination of three decades of remarkable civilizing work by Archbishop Lamy. When Lamy arrived on horseback in Santa Fe in 1851, he found, to his dismay, that he had been assigned to preside over a "desert diocese" recently annexed to the United States and embracing a land area larger than his own native France, with a populace that was 90 percent illiterate. He also soon discovered that even his Spanish parishioners, having lived in a time warp for more than two centuries, had little or no access to the cultural changes that had so altered the outside world.

A sophisticated priest who admired the technological advances that were modernizing his native country, Lamy was disturbed as he surveyed the general destitution that prevailed in his new see. There were few trained priests. The adobe churches were crumbling. Religious instruction and discipline had obvi-ously disintegrated after the Franciscan fathers were forced to withdraw in response to Mexico's becoming an independent, anti-clerical nation in 1821. Paul Horgan used these words in contemplating Lamy's outlook as he evaluated the formidable challenges he faced:

> All was as alien to him as though he had been sent to a missionary station in remotest Africa. It must seem that he had only the primal materials of human society with which to work. In his vocation they were what counted most; but surely he must, when he could, work to bring them the bounties of such worlds as he had left.

Lamy's response reveals that he was not only undaunted but also nurturing expansive ideas about what could be accomplished. He dispatched urgent, incessant appeals for assistance to his superiors in Baltimore and Rome and to the dual offices of the Society for the Propagation of the Faith in Paris and Lyon— and he outlined aims that were both immediate and ambitious. During his first months, he even tried to "borrow" priests from eastern bishops, and he requested loans of funds if outright subsidies were not available.

Lamy's vision encompassed more than improvements of his church's institutions. He favored a wide-ranging approach to growth that would begin with the minds of children and include social advances to make his communities more cohesive and elevate the daily lives and the faith of his communicants. The bishop envisioned the construction of new chapels across his domain. He sought Old World padres (preferably from French seminaries) to replace ill-trained secular priests, and he got action that enabled Franciscan fathers to resume their missionary labors with the Pueblo Indians.

Bishop Lamy's long-range vision encompassed hospitals, an industrial school, and perhaps even a college. However, schools for boys and girls were his first priority. Thus, when he went east in 1852 for a bishops' conference in Baltimore, he stopped at the convent of the Sisters of Loretto in Kentucky and presented a plea for "teaching nuns" to accompany him on his return trip to New Mexico. Six sisters agreed to go, and a few months later the four who had survived a cholera epidemic on the plains opened a school for girls in Santa Fe.

Lamy excelled as a beggar for God. He often assured his associates that "Providence will not abandon us," and to keep his part of the bargain he covered every base and tirelessly removed obstacles he thought were impeding the flow of alms to his people. After a year-long trip to Rome in 1867, for example, he turned homeward with an entourage that included five Italian Jesuits, a priest, and a deacon he had enlisted at the Vatican; two Christian Brothers (members of the Brothers of the Christian Schools); six French seminarians; and an additional group of Lorettine nuns from the motherhouse in Kentucky.

In the male-oriented manner of yesteryear, Paul Horgan and other historians gave the archbishop credit for the transforming work that took place in his diocese and accorded a mere honorable mention to his helpers. It is clear, however, that the sisters Lamy brought to his domain were exceptional doers and that

Lamy wisely gave them broad authority to develop and implement their own plans for community betterment.

Many of the landmark achievements of the Lamy era were an outgrowth of the vision, initiative, and fund-raising skills of these sisters. From the time the Sisters of Loretto appeared on the streets of Santa Fe, opened their first school in January 1853, and commenced their first construction projects, their presence was a symbol of change and hope.

Unlike the bishop (who harbored a prejudice that young Spaniards did not qualify for training as priests), the Lorettine nuns encouraged some of their students to join their order, and in due course one of them, Lucia Perea, became the mother superior of the Convent of Our Lady of Light. These nuns had seemingly boundless energy: by 1869 they had opened schools across New Mexico—in Taos, Mora, Albuquerque, Las Vegas, Las Cruces, Bernalillo, and Socorro—and were spreading their wings to Colorado and parts of Texas.

The successes of the Lorettine sisters helped Bishop Lamy persuade the Sisters of Charity at Cedar Grove in southern Ohio to send four nuns to Santa Fe in the fall of 1865. Two had served as nurses during the Civil War, and the bishop asked them to take over his quarters next to the main cathedral and start New Mexico's first hospital. Within a year, these industrious sisters were operating both a hospital and an orphanage in Santa Fe. And within a few years more, they had opened a hospital in Denver—and they later amazed the miners of Leadville, located on a bleak summit of the Rocky Mountains, by creating another House of Mercy in that boisterous boomtown.

As the 1870s unfolded, the aging bishop not only witnessed the fulfillment of goals he had long cherished but also participated in celebrations that marked a climax of his ministry. The first of these milestones involved the dedication in 1878 of the

Loretto Chapel in Santa Fe. This elegant church, patterned after the Sainte-Chapelle in Paris, was the first Gothic Revival chapel to be built in the American West beyond St. Louis, Missouri.

Not only was the plan for this exquisite church conceived by the Sisters of Loretto and built on the block they had acquired as a site for their convent and schools in the heart of Santa Fe; it was also financed by funds the nuns had raised. As a European ornament on the Santa Fe skyline, it made a statement about change that, in the words of Paul Horgan, "seemed to open the windows of [the bishop's] desert adobe towns upon the world."

The sisters wanted something ennobling as a place of worship and paid handsomely to have stained glass windows designed by a French artist. Shipped by water to St. Louis, these delicate artifacts were then transported across the plains in special wagons and installed under the Lorettine nuns' watchful eyes. When Lieutenant John G. Bourke, a sophisticated army officer from New England, saw this church in 1881, he described it as a "lovely little temple, so sweet, so pure and bright, attesting the constant presence and attention of refined and gentle womanhood."

The consecration of the Loretto Chapel was followed by three developments that brought the Lamy era to a culmination. Once their hospital was established, the Sisters of Charity completed work on an industrial school, which was opened with a festival concert in 1880.

The next year, the indefatigable Lorettine sisters fulfilled another dream by putting the finishing touches on a three-story academy building to house their growing educational endeavors. The overseer of this imposing construction project was the redoubtable mother superior Magdalen Hayden. In explaining the work's rapid completion, Mother Magdalen once recounted, "We started our own brickyard and opened our own quarry . . .

and had our own lime burnt to order and our own lumber sawn by our own natives."

Efforts that produced a third New Mexico landmark were under way at the same time a sheriff killed William Bonney and brought his bloody career to a close. This involved completion by the Christian Brothers of a structure, the tallest adobe building in the Southwest, to house what would be known as St. Michael's College, the territory's first institution of higher learning.

When one puts the achievements of the Lamy epoch in perspective, it is clear that the homicidal activities of Billy the Kid in Lincoln County had as much influence on New Mexico's history and culture as, say, the outcome of a dogfight in a Santa Fe alley.

A Postscript

While doing some of the research for this chapter in 1995, I read the recently published *Oxford History of the American West*. This fresh, comprehensive survey deserved the praise it won from scholars. However, it had a flaw that, for me, highlighted the process by which Wild West myths have distorted the authentic story of the settlement of the West.

When I scanned the index for references to the protagonists featured in this chapter, I was startled by the contrast between the scant attention given to Brigham Young and Archbishop Lamy and the lavish coverage given to the two best-known Wild West outlaws who were their contemporaries:

- Billy the Kid is mentioned in the index more than twenty times, and two full pages are devoted to an account of his mythical life.
- Wyatt Earp is cited in the index twenty-four times, and four pages of text are devoted to his legend.
- Archbishop Lamy's name does not appear in the index, and what he accomplished to advance culture in his ecclesiastical domain is not mentioned in the text.

- Brigham Young receives seven scattered mentions, but there are only sketchy references to decisions he made that guided settlement and civilization in his Great Basin Kingdom.

My convictions about the sources and extent of this gross distortion were fortified later when I delved into *The New Encyclopedia of the American West,* issued in 1998 by Yale University Press. Again, my search turned up numerous incongruities that demonstrate how Wild West "facts" have altered the matrix of western history and displaced historical truths. Here are a few of the egregious incongruities I encountered:

- More space is devoted to the life and times of the latter-day showman William Cody than to the pioneering work of Marcus Whitman, Henry Spalding, Jason Lee, Father Pierre-Jean De Smet, Brigham Young, and Archbishop Lamy.
- Other post–Old West latecomers who are given long, Cody-like biographies are the outlaws Jesse James, the Younger brothers, and the Dalton gang.
- There is no account in the Yale text of the deeds of Francisco Vásquez de Coronado, the Spanish conquistador who explored the Southwest in 1540, or of Father Francisco Silvestre Vélez de Escalante, who mapped the Great Basin in 1776 and probably discovered more western land than did the expedition led by Meriwether Lewis and William Clark.
- The lines used in describing the accomplishments of Juan de Oñate (who, in 1598, founded the first European settlement in the United States) are fewer than those used in presenting the "contributions" to western history of author Louis L'Amour.

In the face of such evidence, need one ask why the founders of the American West are largely forgotten?

A c k n o w l e d g m e n t s

First and last, a bouquet to my wife, Lee, whose ideas and words form part of the tapestry of this book.

For me, one of the joys of writing a wide-ranging book of this kind is the chance to renew old friendships and make new ones that are enduring. This has been one of the enriching experiences of my later years.

I worked on and off on this manuscript for seven years, and some of my counselors of yesteryear are no longer among us, but with warm memories I extend a heartfelt salute to Fray Angelico Chavez, Leonard J. Arrington, George Ellsworth, James Officer, Edmund Ladd, and Lloyd Kiva New. We miss them. Their minds were libraries that nurtured truths about life in the American West.

Two historians who are close friends, Ross Peterson and David Emmons, scanned large sections of my early drafts and presented insights that helped me avoid egregious errors. I tender them special thanks.

Others who graciously perused key sections of chapters and offered valuable counsel are Alvin Josephy Jr., Robert R. Dykstra, David Lavender, Tom Lynn, Gary Topping, Charles S. Peterson, Spense Havlick, Anne M. Butler, Bernard Fontana, Phillip Hocker, Dan Flores, Harold Gilliam, Charles F. Wilkinson, and William Kittredge.

I also owe a special debt to W. Eugene Hollon, who combined

his responses to my questions with trenchant counsel about some verbose sentences.

Finally, I owe a large debt to Jonathan Cobb, my editor. A good editor resolutely challenges his authors to improve and expand the quality of their work. Jonathan wants excellence, and he is tireless in his quest to achieve that goal. He has my profuse thanks for his contributions to this, my final book.

Notes and
Suggested Readings

This book was written for the general reader; the annotations are thus not profuse. Knowing that some of my interpretations will be provocative, I have highlighted here books and articles that will challenge readers to form their own judgments about the events and issues discussed.

Chapter 1. Native Peoples:
The First Forgotten Founders

SUGGESTED READINGS

The following works provide an overview that underscores efforts by latter-day writers to present American history with full consideration of an Indian point of view.

Brown, Dee. *Bury My Heart at Wounded Knee: An Indian History of the American West.* New York: Holt, Rinehart & Winston, 1971.

Deloria, Vine Jr. *Custer Died for Your Sins: An Indian Manifesto.* New York: Macmillan, 1969.

Fey, Harold E., and D'Arcy McNickle. *Indians and Other Americans: Two Ways of Life Meet.* New York: Harper, 1959. Written to counter the move by Congress to terminate the sovereignty of native peoples that gripped Washington, D.C., in the 1950s.

Josephy, Alvin M. Jr. *500 Nations: An Illustrated History of North American Indians*. New York: Knopf, 1994. A superb summation illustrated with a gorgeous array of historical paintings and photographs.

———. *The Indian Heritage of America*. New York: Knopf, 1968.

———. *The Patriot Chiefs: A Chronicle of American Indian Leadership*. New York: Viking Press, 1961.

Wilkinson, Charles F. *American Indians, Time, and the Law: Native Societies in a Modern Constitutional Democracy*. New Haven, Conn.: Yale University Press, 1987.

NOTES

17 "as much natural genius as peoples of Europe": Alexis de Tocqueville, *Democracy in America*, vol. 1 (1835; reprint, New York: Knopf, 1994), 349.

21–24 Of the many volumes written about the Iroquois, I prefer *Apologies to the Iroquois, with a Study of the Mohawks in High Steel* (New York: Farrar, Straus, and Cudahy, 1960), by noted literary critic Edmund Wilson. See also Bruce A. Barton, "Iroquois Confederate Law and the Origins of the U.S. Constitution," *Northeast Indian Quarterly* 3, no. 3 (fall 1986): 4–9.

22 "No people in the world": Edmond Atkin, quoted in Wilbur R. Jacobs, ed., *Indians of the Southern Colonial Frontier: The Edmond Atkin Report and Plan of 1755* (Columbia: University of South Carolina Press, 1954).

24 "the settled doctrine of the law of nations": The significance of Chief Justice Marshall's sweeping landmark opinions is explicated in Charles F. Wilkinson, *American*

Indians, Time, and the Law: Native Societies in a Modern Constitutional Democracy (New Haven, Conn.: Yale University Press, 1987), 55.

25   "At this time there are 22,000 cattle": Presbyterian Church report of 1826, in Harold E. Fey and D'Arcy McNickle, *Indians and Other Americans: Two Ways of Life Meet* (New York: Harper, 1959), 30.

27   "Build a fire under them": John Ehle, *Trail of Tears: The Rise and Fall of the Cherokee Nation* (Garden City, N.Y.: Doubleday, 1988), 220.

28   "it is not now seriously denied": Senator Frelinghuysen's speech is quoted in Thomas Hart Benton, comp., *An Abridgement of the Debates of Congress, from 1789 to 1856*, vol. 10 (Washington, D.C., 1859), 519–525.

29   "They do not have chiefs as in New Spain": Castañeda's complete journal appears in George Parker Winship, "The Coronado Expedition, 1540–1542," in *Fourteenth Annual Report of the Bureau of Ethnology to the Secretary of the Smithsonian Institution, 1892–1893* (Washington, D.C., 1896), 329–613.

Chapter 2. European Settlers: Human Faces, Far-Flung Places

SUGGESTED READINGS

A work that describes the experiences of the Mormons during their winter exodus from Illinois and their overland migration to Utah is Wallace Stegner's *The Gathering of Zion*. For a panoramic presentation of the first phase of Mormon settlement, see Leonard Arrington's *Great Basin Kingdom*. Dr. Arrington also wrote the best biography of Brigham Young, listed in the selections that follow.

Juanita Brooks' pioneering study *The Mountain Meadows*

Massacre led her to write two books about John D. Lee and his families, including her admiring monograph *Emma Lee* and her biography *John D. Lee.*

Arrington, Leonard J. *Brigham Young: American Moses.* New York: Knopf, 1985.

———. *Great Basin Kingdom: An Economic History of the Latter-Day Saints.* Lincoln: University of Nebraska Press, 1966.

Bailey, Paul Dayton. *Jacob Hamblin, Buckskin Apostle.* Los Angeles: Westernlore Press, 1948.

Brooks, Juanita. *Emma Lee.* Logan: Utah State University Press, 1975.

———. *John Doyle Lee: Zealot, Pioneer-Builder, Scapegoat.* Glendale, Calif.: A. H. Clark, 1962.

———. *The Mountain Meadows Massacre.* Stanford, Calif.: Stanford University Press, 1950.

Corbett, Pearson H. *Jacob Hamblin, the Peacemaker.* Salt Lake City, Utah: Deseret, 1952.

Stegner, Wallace. *The Gathering of Zion: The Story of the Mormon Trail.* New York: McGraw-Hill, 1964.

NOTES

I gleaned most of the facts about my wife's and my ancestors from privately published family histories, journals kept by some of the protagonists, and memoirs composed by their children.

53   "This man Hamblin": Thomas Edwin Farish, *History of Arizona by Thomas Edwin Farish, Arizona Historian,* vol. 5 (San Francisco: Filmer Brothers Electrotype Company, 1918), 329.

63–70   Correspondence and other documents concerning my conclusions about the Mountain Meadows massacre are in my papers in the Stewart Lee Udall Collection, University of Arizona Library, Special Collections.

Chapter 3. Explorers and Fur Trappers

SUGGESTED READINGS

Chittenden, Hiram M. *The American Fur Trade of the Far West.* New York: F. P. Harper, 1902.

Hafen, LeRoy R., ed. *French Fur Traders and Voyageurs in the American West: Twenty-Five Biographical Sketches.* Spokane, Wash.: A. H. Clark, 1995. It is revealing that Canada never had a De Voto who transformed its western explorers into visionary "agents of empire."

Stegner, Wallace. *The Uneasy Chair: A Biography of Bernard De Voto.* Garden City, N.Y.: Doubleday, 1974.

Unruh, John D. Jr. *The Plains Across: The Overland Emigrants and the Trans-Mississippi West, 1840–60.* Urbana: University of Illinois Press, 1979. This fact-filled study debunks elements of De Voto's romantic "histories."

Utley, Robert M. *A Life Wild and Perilous: Mountain Men and the Paths to the Pacific.* New York: Henry Holt, 1997.

NOTES

I had serious misgivings when I decided to pick a quarrel with Bernard De Voto. I was reluctant because he was a hero to me and my colleagues in Congress for his combative battle-essays in *Harper's* magazine, which revived the conservation movement in the decade after the end of World War II. I was also uneasy because two choice friends of mine—Wallace Stegner and Arthur Schlesinger Jr.—had been members of his circle at Harvard University and esteemed him as a mentor who fought for causes they believed in.

79   "On every page . . . we hear the sound history makes": Wallace Stegner, *The Uneasy Chair: A Biography of Bernard De Voto* (Garden City, N.Y.: Doubleday, 1974).

81   "Drums should have rolled": Bernard De Voto, *The Year of Decision, 1846* (Boston: Little, Brown, 1943), 462.

82   "sudden acceleration of social energies": Ibid., 18.

84   De Voto's passages characterizing the western natives as depraved: Ibid., 249–250.

85   "as he would have stepped on piss-ants": Ibid., 63.

86   "The extent of Indian attacks . . . has been greatly exaggerated": John D. Unruh Jr., *The Plains Across: The Overland Emigrants and the Trans-Mississippi West, 1840–60* (Urbana: University of Illinois Press, 1979), 385–386.

88   "The missionaries were vortices": Bernard De Voto, *Across the Wide Missouri* (Boston: Houghton Mifflin, 1947), 371.

90   De Voto's begrudging praise for Brigham Young: De Voto, *Year of Decision*, 454.

Chapter 4. The Religion Factor in Western Settlement

SUGGESTED READINGS

The paramount role churches and their missionaries played in western settlement has too often been relegated to the margins in the interpretations of modern historians. This chapter represents an effort to correct the record by recounting the irrefragable contributions of westering religionists, whose work laid the foundations of the modern West.

Sydney Ahlstrom's *Religious History of the American People* is a magisterial overview that traces the influence of religion on American life in the eighteenth and nineteenth centuries. In *Religion and the American Mind*, the late Alan Heimert demonstrates the influence "protesting" Protestant preaching had in generating the spirit of insubordination that animated the

American Revolution. William Lee Miller's *Arguing about Slavery* reminds us that it was the moral passion generated by theological arguments of Protestant preachers in the 1830s that created the abolitionist fervor that made the Civil War inevitable.

Ahlstrom, Sydney H. *A Religious History of the American People.* New Haven, Conn.: Yale University Press, 1972.

Heimert, Alan. *Religion and the American Mind, from the Great Awakening to the Revolution.* Cambridge, Mass.: Harvard University Press, 1966.

Killoren, John J. *"Come, Blackrobe": De Smet and the Indian Tragedy.* Norman: University of Oklahoma Press, 1994. A sensitive account of Father Pierre-Jean De Smet.

Miller, William Lee. *Arguing about Slavery: The Great Battle in the United States Congress.* New York: Knopf, 1996.

NOTES

91   "Upon my arrival in the United States": Alexis de Tocqueville, quoted in Sydney H. Ahlstrom, *A Religious History of the American People* (New Haven, Conn.: Yale University Press, 1972), 386.

95   Herbert Bolton's comments about Father Kino: Ibid., 45.

98   Bolton's summary of Father Serra's achievements: Ibid., 45.

102   "Religion in America takes no direct part": Alexis de Tocqueville, *Democracy in America,* vol. 1 (1835; reprint, New York: Knopf, 1994), 305.

106   "[Those] who had made the monumental journey": David Lavender, *Westward Vision: The Story of the Oregon Trail* (New York: McGraw-Hill, 1963), 265.

107   "It represents one of the few regional economies": Leonard J. Arrington, *Great Basin Kingdom: An Economic*

History of the Latter-Day Saints (Lincoln: University of
Nebraska Press, 1966), vii.

108   "a witness to the possible social potency": Ahlstrom, *A
Religious History*, 407.

Chapter 5. The Manifest Destiny Morass

SUGGESTED READINGS

No catchphrase has exerted such a mesmerizing influence over
American thought as the slippery slogan "Manifest Destiny." Too
many historians mouth it as a mantra, and for a century and a half
politicians and superpatriots have wafted it as a magic wand to ward
off criticisms of imperialistic excesses of American expansionism.

Merk, Frederick. *Manifest Destiny and Mission in American History: A Reinterpretation.* New York: Knopf, Random House,
  1963. Merk, a Harvard University historian, deflated the messianic "doctrine" of Manifest Destiny in his definitive study of
  the subject. Unfortunately, however, the concept had become
  so embedded in American language and folklore that Merk's
  message has largely been ignored by both scholars and laymen.
  Readers who want to wrestle with the truth about this mischievous axiom should study Merk's text.
Ohrt, Wallace. *Defiant Peacemaker: Nicholas Trist in the Mexican
  War.* College Station: Texas A&M University Press, 1997. Historian Wallace Ohrt examines the life of self-appointed nego-
  tiator Nicholas Trist and his insubordinate caper that produced
  the treaty that concluded the Mexican War. He depicts Trist as
  a man of principle willing to sacrifice his career to do justice to
  a defeated foe.

NOTES

111   "Manifest Destiny and imperialism were traps": Freder-
        ick Merk, *Manifest Destiny and Mission in American His-*

tory: A Reinterpretation (New York: Knopf, Random House, 1963), 24.

111 "[It is America's] manifest destiny to overspread": John L. O'Sullivan, "The True Title," editorial in the *New York Morning News*, 1845, quoted in Merk, *Manifest Destiny and Mission*.

120 "Instead . . . an appeal has been made to your worst passions": This and other statements by Albert Gallatin are quoted ibid., 262 et seq.

Chapter 6. California Gold Fever: Fact and Fancy

Suggested Readings

It is impossible for any observer to describe the details of a stampede, and the every-man-for-himself human maelstrom called the California gold rush is no exception. Among the vast, ever-expanding literature on the California gold rush, I found the following books particularly useful.

Gutiérrez, Ramón, and Richard J. Orsi, eds. *Contested Eden: California before the Gold Rush*. Berkeley: University of California Press, 1998.

Holliday, J. S. *The World Rushed In: The California Gold Rush Experience*. New York: Simon and Schuster, 1981. The best, most comprehensive study of the California gold rush.

Jackson, Donald D. *Gold Dust*. New York: Knopf, 1980.

Kroeber, Theodora, and Robert F. Heizer. *Almost Ancestors: The First Californians*. San Francisco: Sierra Club Books, 1968. The dark side of the California gold rush is given short shrift in most histories. It is revealing, for example, that one of the most searing accounts of the wanton slaughter of the native peoples of the Golden State was not published until 1968.

Marks, Paula Mitchell. *Precious Dust: The American Gold Rush Era, 1848–1900*. New York: Morrow, 1994.

Paul, Rodman W. *California Gold: The Beginning of Mining in the Far West*. Cambridge, Mass.: Harvard University Press, 1947.

NOTES

123   "[Mining] is perhaps the most disadvantageous lottery in the world": Adam Smith, *An Inquiry into the Nature and Causes of the Wealth of Nations* (New York: Random House, Modern Library Edition, 1937), 529.

130   "lucky to make expenses": Paula Mitchell Marks, *Precious Dust: The American Gold Rush Era, 1848–1900* (New York: Morrow, 1994), 30.

130   "tatterdemalion refuges": Donald D. Jackson, *Gold Dust* (New York: Knopf, 1980), 302.

131   "The sweetest illusions are lost": Ibid., 302.

133   "one great cesspool": Marks, *Precious Dust*, 202.

136   "The state's best farming land": William G. Robbins, *Colony and Empire: The Capitalist Transformation of the American West* (Lawrence: University Press of Kansas, 1994).

139   "degraded objects of filth": Jackson, *Gold Dust*, 267–268.

139   "as close to genocide": Alvin M. Josephy Jr., *500 Nations: An Illustrated History of North American Indians* (New York: Knopf, 1994), 347.

Chapter 7. Bootstrap Capitalism in the Old West

SUGGESTED READINGS

Readers who want to understand the contours of Old West capitalism and the paramount importance of communal cooperation and individual initiative during the settlement period will want to peruse the following works.

Bonadio, Felice A. *A. P. Giannini, Banker of America.* Berkeley: University of California Press, 1994. This should be read by those interested in the origin and ramifications of indigenous western capitalism.

Emmons, David. *The Butte Irish: Class and Ethnicity in an American Mining Town, 1875–1925.* Urbana: University of Illinois Press, 1989. A vivid social history that illustrates the perils of overgeneralizing about western development.

May, Dean L. *Three Frontiers: Family, Land, and Society in the American West, 1850–1900.* New York: Cambridge University Press, 1994. An excellent social history of western development.

Milner, Clyde A. II, Carol A. O'Connor, and Martha A. Sandweiss, eds. *The Oxford History of the American West.* New York: Oxford University Press, 1994. A nuanced perspective of pre–Civil War development can be found in three essays in this volume: Keith L. Bryant, "Entering the Global Economy," p. 195; Richard White, "Animals and Enterprise," p. 237; and Allan G. Bogue, "An Agricultural Empire," p. 275.

Robbins, William G. *Colony and Empire: The Capitalist Transformation of the American West.* Lawrence: University Press of Kansas, 1994. In this paean to Big Capitalism, Robbins creates confusion by ignoring initiatives of early frontier folk that paved the way for large-scale enterprises.

NOTES

146   "the most fundamental of all human activities": George Ellsworth, letter to the author, 1997.

151   "hard to exaggerate the rootlessness": Keith L. Bryant, "Entering the Global Economy," in Clyde A. Milner II, Carol A. O'Connor, and Martha A. Sandweiss, eds., *The Oxford History of the American West* (New York: Oxford University Press, 1994), 204.

151   "a senseless, rootless place": Mary Halleck Foote, quoted

in Richard White, *"It's Your Misfortune and None of My Own": A New History of the American West* (Norman: University of Oklahoma Press, 1991), 307.

151 "jerky, wasteful and . . . evanescent development": Allan Nevins, *The Emergence of Modern America, 1865–1878* (New York: Macmillan, 1927), 134.

152 "the Guggenheims and the Goulds": William G. Robbins, *Colony and Empire: The Capitalist Transformation of the American West* (Lawrence: University Press of Kansas, 1994), 33.

157 "a set of social values": David Emmons, *The Butte Irish: Class and Ethnicity in an American Mining Town, 1875–1925* (Urbana: University of Illinois Press, 1989).

157 "everything the West was not supposed to be": Ibid.

158 "no rivals among the mining cities": Ibid., 13.

159–60 "more driven by dreams of building something"; "the Irish ran everything"; "an antidote to the historical myth of a Protestant, rural West": David Emmons, letter to the author, 1996.

160 "crafting the everyday": Janet L. Finn, *Tracing the Veins: Of Copper, Culture, and Community from Butte to Chuquicamata* (Berkeley: University of California Press, 1998), 147–176.

Chapter 8. The Wild West and the Wrenching of the American Chronicle

SUGGESTED READINGS

The hard-line argument that the West was a place where gunfighters were prevalent and "the threat of gunplay was pervasive" is presented in works of senior western historian Richard Maxwell Brown.

One finds a counter-thesis in the writings of cultural historian Richard Slotkin. In *Gunfighter Nation* and other volumes, Slotkin examines the baleful influence of western films on American culture and on American glorification of violence.

In an effort to slow the mesmerizing influence of Hollywood's juggernaut, in the 1960s two forthright historians, Robert R. Dykstra and W. Eugene Hollon, separately demonstrated how western history was being mangled by the media. Dykstra's *Cattle Towns* debunked the myth that Dodge City and other central Kansas locations that served as railheads for Texas drovers experienced virtually continuous handgun violence. See also his incisive essay titled "Field Notes."

Hollon conducted the first general survey of this subject, and in *Frontier Violence* he demonstrates that, overall, there was more violence in American cities during the nineteenth century than in frontier communities. Hollon's thesis was buttressed the same year by Richard Bartlett in *The New Country*.

A scholar who has an uncommon feel for the frontier and for the lives people lived in this environment is Elliott West. All of his western history books are first-rate.

Bartlett, Richard A. *The New Country: A Social History of the American Frontier, 1776–1890.* New York: Oxford University Press, 1974.

Dykstra, Robert R. *The Cattle Towns.* New York: Knopf, 1968.

———. "Field Notes: Overdosing on Dodge City." *Western Historical Quarterly* (winter 1996): 505.

Hollon, W. Eugene. *Frontier Violence: Another Look.* New York: Oxford University Press, 1974.

Slotkin, Richard. *Gunfighter Nation: The Myth of the Frontier in Twentieth-Century America.* New York: Atheneum, 1992.

West, Elliott. *The Contested Plains: Indians, Goldseekers, and the Rush to Colorado.* Lawrence: University Press of Kansas, 1998.

———. *The Way to the West: Essays on the Central Plains.* Albuquerque: University of New Mexico Press, 1995.

NOTES

165   "Despite all of the mythologizing": Robert R. Dykstra, "Field Notes: Overdosing on Dodge City," *Western Historical Quarterly* (winter 1996): 505.

166–67   "essential safety"; "fatal trail confrontations . . . usually prompted by emigrant insults": These and other quotations are from John D. Unruh Jr., *The Plains Across: The Overland Emigrants and the Trans-Mississippi West, 1840–60* (Urbana: University of Illinois Press, 1979), 185, 379 et seq., 386, 408.

168   "a perpetually violent and lawless place": Richard White, *"It's Your Misfortune and None of My Own": A New History of the American West* (Norman: University of Oklahoma Press, 1991), 329.

169   "Personal violence . . . confined to very narrow social milieus": Ibid., 332.

174   "Marlboro man": Robert R. Dykstra, "Field Notes: Overdosing on Dodge City," *Western Historical Quarterly* (winter 1996): 511.

179   "They won because they outnumbered the enemy": Robert M. Utley, *The Lance and the Shield: The Life and Times of Sitting Bull* (New York: Henry Holt, 1993), 162.

179–80   "The real conquerors": Robert M. Utley and Wilcomb E. Washburn, *The American Heritage History of the Indian Wars* (New York: American Heritage, 1977), 329.

184   Cody as "national caretaker for western authenticity": Anne M. Butler, in *The Oxford History of the American West*, ed. Clyde A. Milner II, Carol A. O'Connor, and

Martha A. Sandweiss (New York: Oxford University Press, 1994), 781.

186   "art designed for the widest possible audience": William Kittredge, in Stewart L. Udall, Patricia Nelson Limerick, and Charles F. Wilkinson, *Beyond the Mythic West* (Salt Lake City: Peregrine Smith Books, in association with the Western Governor's Association, 1990), 138.

188–89 "If you start reading around": Ibid., 147.

Chapter 9. The Wild West and the Settlers: Contrasting Visions

SUGGESTED READINGS

The saga of European settlement in what is now the United States of America began in New Mexico, and a master historian, the late Paul Horgan, told this four-century story in two magnificent books, *Great River* and *Lamy of Santa Fe.*

Two works separated by a half-century chronicle the story of Mormon pioneering in Arizona. James H. McClintock's *Mormon Settlement in Arizona* is an account written by a journalist who came to Arizona in 1879. Historian Charles S. Peterson adds rich detail to this story in *Take Up Your Mission.*

Horgan, Paul. *Great River: The Rio Grande in North American History.* New York: Holt, Rinehart & Winston, 1954.

———. *Lamy of Santa Fe: His Life and Times.* New York: Farrar, Straus and Giroux, 1975.

McClintock, James H. *Mormon Settlement in Arizona: A Record of Peaceful Conquest of the Desert.* Phoenix, Ariz., 1921; reprint, Tucson: University of Arizona Press, 1985.

Peterson, Charles S. *Take Up Your Mission: Mormon Colonizing along the Little Colorado River, 1870–1900.* Tucson: University of Arizona Press, 1973.

NOTES

191   "a far more civilized, more peaceful, and safer place": W. Eugene Hollon, *Frontier Violence: Another Look* (New York: Oxford University Press, 1974).

193   "The public sympathized with the Clantons": Odie B. Faulk, *Arizona: A Short History* (Norman: University of Oklahoma Press, 1970), 178.

193   "when they were assaulted": Bert M. Fireman, *Arizona: Historic Land* (New York: Knopf, 1982), 199.

195   "found more than they bargained for in Tombstone": Thomas E. Sheridan, *Arizona: A History* (Tucson: University of Arizona Press, 1995), 154.

195   "averted bloodshed": Charles S. Peterson, *Take Up Your Mission: Mormon Colonizing along the Little Colorado River, 1870–1900* (Tucson: University of Arizona Press, 1973).

195   "The West was won by toil": Bert Fireman, in Lawrence Clark Powell, *Arizona: A Bicentennial History* (New York: Norton, 1976), ix.

197   "might well have vanished into oblivion": Robert M. Utley, *Billy the Kid: A Short and Violent Life* (Lincoln: University of Nebraska Press, 1989), 198.

198   "implanted in the hundreds of [so-called] histories": Ibid., 199.

199   "a youthful murderer": Paul Horgan, *Lamy of Santa Fe: His Life and Times* (New York: Farrar, Straus and Giroux, 1975), 397.

200   "All was as alien to him": Ibid., 118.

203   "seemed to open the windows": Ibid., 394.

203   "lovely little temple": Mary J. Straw, *Loretto: The Sisters and Their Santa Fe Chapel* (Santa Fe, N.M.: Loretto Chapel, 1983), 53.

Index

STEWART L. UDALL was elected to four terms as congressman from Arizona before being appointed by John F. Kennedy to serve as secretary of the interior, a position he held for eight years during the administrations of Presidents Kennedy and Lyndon B. Johnson. During his tenure as interior secretary, Udall played a major role in enlarging the concept of the national park system, fostering protection of wilderness areas, and helping to catalyze the emergence of the environmental movement.

An Arizona native who grew up in a community not unlike those of settlers he describes in *The Forgotten Founders*, Udall is a student of history, an outdoorsman, a proponent of the arts, and a champion of the rights of Navajo Indian uranium miners. He has lectured widely at universities and to a variety of other audiences on natural resources, ecology, and history. He now lives in Santa Fe, New Mexico.

Udall is the author of many books. Among these, his first, *The Quiet Crisis* (1963), was a best-seller that brought many conservation issues to national attention; *To the Inland Empire: Coronado and Our Spanish Legacy* (1987) told the story of early Hispanic contributions to U.S. history; and *The Myths of August: A Personal Exploration of Our Tragic Cold War Affair with the Atom* (1994) was a critique of atomic research and weaponry and the forces behind their promotion.

DAVID M. EMMONS is a professor of history at the University of Montana, Missoula. He is the author of *Garden in the Grasslands: Boomer Literature of the Central Great Plains* (1971) and *The Butte Irish: Class and Ethnicity in an American Mining Town, 1875–1925* (1989), as well as many articles and essays on the history of the American West.